it up in
hanical
namics
73. His
Mama
by Tim

quickly
r made
von the
he best
mising
British

by the
orrow?
and A
ny. The
seasons
980 the
Bruce
around
ased in
(1982),
on and
1989.
0.
1, Los
es was
made
Theatre

Centre in 1994 and has also been filmed. *Dead White Males* was first produced in Sydney in 1995 and in the UK in 1996. *Heretic* premiered in Sydney in 1996. His revised working of *Jugglers Three* was premiered by Sydney Theatre Company and toured nationally in 1997 under the title *Third World Blues*.

David Williamson has won the Australian Film Institute film script award for *Petersen* (1974), *Don's Party* (1976), *Gallipoli* (1981) and *Travelling North* (1987) and has won eleven Australian Writers' Guild AWGIE Awards. He lives on Queensland's Sunshine Coast with his writer wife Kristin Williamson.

merely keep functioning in the midst of a maelstrom of other
people's competing egos, needs and agendas. And that the impetus
for us to keep going is, unfortunately, more often anxiety and fear
than "happiness". The best and most honest drama tells us just how
hard it is, and what courage it often takes, to merely keep our heads
above water in the churning social sea in which we all must swim.

After the Ball, despite the fact that we will often invite the
laughter of recognition, is not essentially about happiness. When my
mother was dying, I tried to talk her through that last hour without
knowing whether she could hear me. The nurse said, "Probably—
hearing's the last thing to go." I talked to her in the sort of way my
character, Stephen, talks to his dying mother in the play. Given this
admission, is the drama I write simply a transcription of life, and is
this latest play my most blatant bit of life borrowing? Yes and no.
It's certainly close in many areas. My purpose in writing it *was*
partly to try and make sense of the family I grew up in and the
impact that family had had on me.

It *is* an attempt, among other things, to look at the sadness and
humour that occur when two partners as mismatched as my parents
are bound together for life in holy matrimony in an era in which
divorce was all but unthinkable. (It is *not*, however, a play on the
social issue of marriage and its limitations. I recently attended the
funeral of my mother's sister who had a marriage that was
characterised by fifty-five years of love and respect.)

It's also a play about what happens to an eleven-year-old when
the capacity of the human psyche for duplicity is starkly revealed to
him. Here again I *have* borrowed from life. At the age of eleven my
parents had an argument so ferocious that the end of the marriage
seemed imminent. My mother raced from the room, apparently in
tears. I followed her, worried, to the laundry where, to my
astonishment, I found her giggling to herself. She didn't see me and I
crept away; but many, many years later, after more than one drink on
both our parts, I plucked up the courage to ask her about the
incident. Her reply was, I think, astonishing in its directness and
candour. You're going to have to read the play to find out what it
was, but it's a reply that caused me, and my character Stephen, forty
years on, to re-evaluate the nature of our parents' relationship. But in
the same way as my play *Don's Party* is not the transcription of a

tape recording of an actual party, *After the Ball* is not a literal transcription of my life in my family.

The play is shaped to sharpen the conflicts and their consequences beyond the strictly autobiographical. I have created a Stephen who is more declamatory, vulnerable and desperate than I think I am, and he has a sister who survives the marital warfare more robustly than I think my brother and I did. I did this to make the drama stronger and the issues debated more sharply contested. In the play, Stephen's sister, Judy, also discovers that her mother is taunting her father, but at seventeen, and with different sympathies, it has a totally different impact on her life.

The play diverges from life in order to suggest that the same seminal event, interpreted differently by the two siblings, can have vastly different outcomes. On Stephen's part it helps to engender a fear of torment and a distrust of humanity. He has decided, in his sister's words, that the "world is cruel and heartless and he's closed down all connections". Judy has remained open and warm and compassionate, and this difference feeds into the way they see the future of Australia itself. Stephen believes that Europe has generated a priceless artistic heritage and has relocated himself there permanently rather than live in an Australia that he sees as progressively turning its back on its heritage. His sister Judy believes that Australia is an exciting country that is forging a new identity that is not European, not Asian, but something uniquely its own, and she could no more leave it than stop breathing.

I've been asked, and indeed during the writing of the play I had to ask myself, whether I identified with the viewpoint of Stephen or that of Judy. The truthful answer is that I identified with both. This is often what I find happening when I write. The more pessimistic and optimistic sides of my psyche are split into different characters for the sake of heightened drama. I like writing about situations in which I'm never quite sure what I believe or what I feel because it enables me to inhabit a range of characters with sympathy and conviction.

Writing this particular play has made me face up to the question of whether my life's preoccupation—to analyse people in conflict— has arisen from my own family experience. My wife Kristin says there is no doubt that this is so. When she first met my parents she was astonished by their non-stop repartee. My brother and I might have been turning white with anguish, but she found it intriguing and entertaining. The power of drama, unlike film, which usually focusses on a central protagonist with whom we uncritically "identify", is that the dramatist can keep an ironic focus on *all* of the characters and ask the audience to make up their own minds about who are the good guys and the bad guys. This, hopefully, will be true of *After the Ball*. I always invite the audiences and readers of my plays to laugh at the egotism and blindness of my characters, but at the same time to remain sympathetic to the fact, as Kristin was to my brother and me, that the characters themselves aren't having fun. The truth is we *all* behave foolishly a lot of the time. It is truly, I think, part of the human condition.

Marcus Beach
July 1997

A Classic Text

Robyn Nevin

David Williamson entrusted his new play to me in May 1996. He gave Queensland Theatre Company, of which I was artistic director, the national rights to *After the Ball*, allowing us to present the world premiere in our Brisbane season and tour the production to other states. I would direct the play. David did not request a dramaturg: he was satisfied to work through the various drafts in his own time offering each one to me for my responses. We worked through five drafts in this way. The casting process too was slow and thoughtful and thorough. It included close consultation with David, who knows the Australian community of actors very well.

Theory is fascinating but talent, skill and experience are better. To act is to do. *After the Ball* suggested immediate action to me—no sitting around a table analysing the play. I was confident of my cast, of my own ability to bring the Williamson experience to the floor and confident that the life experience we had all accrued would inform the work. We were all from families, we had all left home, returned, seen our parents ageing, and, if we had not all been exposed to the entire three decades covered in the text, we were acutely aware of the debate around the issue of the changing face of Australia. This last had been raging at an escalating pace since David Williamson had sent me the first draft.

I started blocking on the second day and ran the play at the end of the first week. The absorption process over the duration of the four-week rehearsal period is an important part of the actor's experience of knowing the play, knowing the journey of the characters on whose behalf the actors will breathe and speak. My main concern in realising David's play was to observe his rhythms. I have never yet seen a production of a Williamson in which this has been satisfactorily achieved. I know from acting in his plays that his rhythms are critical to the "success" of the whole. If all the actors can manage to reject their own personal idiosyncratic rhythms (as you must when approaching classical texts) the production will achieve a sense of unity. It will have a greater confidence and clarity. It provides a solid structural base which will prove indestructible in the face of the welcome if raucous laughter of an adoring audience, and the usual problems of actors working over a long run. My other concern was to leave value judgements to the audience. It is critical for the actor to set aside his or her judgement of a character to play the person as written. My productions start with this assumption, which leaves the way clear for those who buy tickets to experience the play, to shape their own conclusions about the characters and the content.

My own early experience working continuously on classic texts (an experience only possible with state companies and now sadly a rare thing) gave me the technical awareness and skill essential to all acting. It equipped me for the Williamson style. Williamson sets real challenges for an actor. His writing demands fierce concentration, high energy, vocal dexterity, mental agility, absolute precision, complete control over the material, and all of this achieved with apparent ease, relaxation and supreme confidence. Once mastered the work is a joy to perform. But you cannot take your eye off the ball for a moment.

As a master craftsman David Williamson is at his peak in *After the Ball*. He made us acutely aware of the ways in which he had structured the dialogue in a scene to build to a laugh and observing the rhythms served the inherent comedy. To observe the psychological truth of each moment became our primary concern. In the final outcome the confident structure we worked so hard to achieve has enabled the play to survive the energetic and almost enveloping audience responses. The production, true to the Williamson style, retained its integrity.

Brisbane
July 1997

To the memory of my parents
Elvie May and Edwin Keith David Williamson,
loved and missed by their two sons,
and finally at peace.

Left to right: Gael Ballantyne as Claire, Carol Burns as Kate (younger) and
Sally McKenzie as Maureen in the 1997 Queensland Theatre Company
production. (Photo: Rob MacColl)

After the Ball was first produced by Queensland Theatre Company at the Suncorp Theatre, Brisbane, on 3 July 1997 with the following cast:

KATE MACCRAE (older)	Penny Everingham
JUDY MACCRAE (older)	Jennifer Flowers
STEPHEN MACCRAE (older)	Bille Brown
RON MACCRAE	Max Gillies
KATE MACCRAE (younger)	Carol Burns
JUDY MACCRAE (younger) / NURSE	Melissa McMahon
STEPHEN MACCRAE (younger)	Anthony Weigh
CLAIRE CUMMINS	Gael Ballantyne
MAUREEN DONANHUE	Sally McKenzie

Director, Robyn Nevin
Designer, Bill Haycock
Lighting Designer, David Walters,
Music, Max Lambert

CHARACTERS

KATE MACCRAE (older)
JUDY MACCRAE (older)
STEPHEN MACCRAE (older)
RON MACCRAE
KATE MACCRAE (younger)
JUDY MACCRAE (younger)
STEPHEN MACCRAE (younger)
CLAIRE CUMMINS
MAUREEN DONAHUE
NURSE

ACKNOWLEDGEMENT

The excerpts from Terence Rattigan's *French Without Tears* quoted in the rehearsal scene on pages 24-28 are reproduced with kind permission of Nick Hern Books, London.

ACT ONE

Dark stage. On a screen the date 1996 is projected. This facility is used throughout the play to pinpoint the year in which the action takes place.

Lights slowly up to reveal KATE, *in her seventies, lying in a hospice bed with a morphine drip in her arm.* JUDY, *her daughter, a woman of fifty-one, sits next to the bed.* KATE *becomes conscious and looks at* JUDY.

KATE: Is he coming?

JUDY: He rang from the airport. He hired a car and he's on his way.

> KATE *sighs and drops off to sleep.* STEPHEN *enters quietly.* JUDY *looks up at her brother, who is one year older than she is. She gets up and embraces him with tears in her eyes.* KATE *wakes and stares at her son.*

KATE: You came!

STEPHEN: Of course I came.

KATE: You came.

> STEPHEN *kisses his mother. She grabs his hand and clutches it with all her remaining strength, then sighs and lapses back into unconsciousness.* STEPHEN *is beckoned out of earshot by his sister and moves away from his mother's bed.*

JUDY: Sometimes she's awake and can hear what you're saying.

STEPHEN: Is she in pain?

JUDY: She says she isn't. It's a very aggressive cancer but she's on a heavy morphine drip.

STEPHEN: Her mind hasn't gone. She definitely recognised me.

JUDY: She can still be quite lucid for a short stretch.

STEPHEN: Sorry I didn't come earlier.

JUDY: You got here in time.

STEPHEN: The bloody doctors were infuriating. All they would say is that it could be a month or it could be days. How are Ray and the kids?

JUDY: They're not kids any more.

STEPHEN: No I guess they're not.

JUDY: They're fine. Your family?

STEPHEN: Fine. Do we have to stay in her house at that retirement village?

JUDY: It's only minutes from here. We could get a call in the night and I don't want to be an hour and a half away.

STEPHEN: I'm not staying there for a month!

JUDY: The nurse I trust says it's just a matter of days.

STEPHEN: I've got to be in Spain at the end of next week. If she hangs on I'll just have to go and come back.

JUDY: [*tersely*] Maybe you might have to cancel Spain. Death doesn't always fit in with schedules.

STEPHEN: Are there any decent hotels nearby?

JUDY: No. Is it that horrific to have to briefly share a house with your sister?

STEPHEN: That retirement village freaks me out.

JUDY: You've only been there twice.

STEPHEN: The walking frames were bad enough, but the thing that really got to me were those gliding electric wheelchairs.

JUDY: It's quite a cheerful village.

STEPHEN: Cheerful? Please. They send a guy around each morning yelling, "Bring out your dead."

JUDY: [*getting up to go*] If I don't get back there and rest I'll be one of them. [*She indicates their mother.*] She sleeps through the night, so there's no point staying after six or so. Do you remember the way?

STEPHEN: I'll follow the ambulances.

JUDY: Pick up some Chinese food or something.

STEPHEN: Watch those wheelchairs. You can't hear them coming and their drivers can't see.

They embrace. JUDY *has tears in her eyes.*

JUDY: [*indicating* KATE] I didn't think it'd make me this—upset. I'm
glad you came.

> *She leaves.* STEPHEN *watches her go, then turns and sits by his
> mother's bed.* KATE *opens her eyes.*

KATE: I'll be with your father again soon.

> *Pause.*

Whether he likes it or not.

STEPHEN: Do you need anything? Water?

KATE: Music.

> STEPHEN *moves across to the CD player and selects a disc.*

Not that one. The other. Did you hear me? I'll be with your father
again soon.

STEPHEN: Yes.

KATE: Whether he likes it or not. Probably not. Third track.

> STEPHEN *nods and puts it on. The music starts. It's "After the
> Ball is Over"—a redigitalised version of an old thirties
> recording.* STEPHEN *and* KATE *listen to it.* STEPHEN *looks at
> his mother who drifts off to sleep.*

*   *   *   *   *   *

1996. Later that evening. STEPHEN *is with his sister in their mother's
living room, a tidy but soulless modern unit in a retirement village.
It's about 9pm. Photo albums and packets of photos that didn't make
the album are strewn around the floor, together with a cuttings
album and various metal boxes containing the family documents.
The screen on which dates are projected is also used to allow the
audience to see the particular photo or document that is being
scrutinised.* JUDY *is thumbing through the photo album and* STEPHEN
is looking over her shoulder. JUDY *stops at one and they both look at
it. On the screen we see a black and white shot of their mother as a
young bride on the morning of the wedding. She's a very beautiful
nineteen year old in a full bridal dress and veil. She's holding a
large bunch of flowers and the train of her dress is held by a pretty*

young girl of six or seven. The backdrop, her parents' house, is unmistakably shabby—a cobbled brick garden and a latticework verandah behind with slats missing.

JUDY: God you forget.

STEPHEN: How beautiful she was?

JUDY: No. The house she grew up in. It explains a lot.

The next shot they stop at is of their parents after the wedding ceremony. Their father, RON, handsome in his morning suit, and their mother radiant.

STEPHEN: The agony begins.

JUDY: Deep down I think they loved each other.

STEPHEN *looks at his sister, surprised.*

Maybe not "loved", but certainly "needed". I know Mum was always teasing Dad—

STEPHEN: Teasing? *Tormenting.*

JUDY: *He* gave *her* a hard time too.

STEPHEN: All he ever did was defend himself.

JUDY: He treated her as if she was stupid. Which she wasn't.

STEPHEN: The madder she got him the more she enjoyed it. Up to the time I caught her giggling—-

JUDY: [*wearily nodding*] In the laundry—

STEPHEN: —in the laundry, I thought she was just as upset as he was. And there she was laughing her head off. What was I supposed to make of that? At the age of eleven?

JUDY: People don't torment other people without a reason.

STEPHEN: Don't they? You try and survive in a schoolyard when you're six inches shorter than you should have been.

JUDY: For God's sake. Your hormones kicked in a bit late and occasionally you got teased.

STEPHEN: You *still* have no idea what my school years were like, do you? Miss Well Adjusted, Miss Bright and Chirpy, Miss Ring a Ring a Rosie—everybody's friend.

JUDY: [*irritated*] Everybody gets teased in the schoolyard.

STEPHEN: Yeah, yeah.

JUDY: It wasn't that bad. You were coming top of your class every year.

STEPHEN: That made it worse.

JUDY: You had friends.

STEPHEN: One. The other outcast.

JUDY: Spare me the agony.

STEPHEN: You want to know how bad it got? It got to the point where I didn't want to be alive. You want to know why I felt warmer about Dad than I ever will about our mother? At least he noticed that I was going through some sort of crisis.

JUDY: Did he ever *do* anything?

STEPHEN: Yes he did. And at the times when it really counted.

JUDY: Such as?

STEPHEN: My first school dance. The only girl I got up the courage to ask laughed in my face. I was genuinely suicidal. He knew something was wrong and he just sat with me and told me that I was brighter than any of them and that I'd have the last laugh in the long run.

JUDY: Well you have, so stop whingeing.

STEPHEN: I'm just trying to explain why I didn't particularly enjoy seeing Dad tormented.

JUDY: The truth is *Mum* was the vulnerable one in that relationship.

STEPHEN: Vulnerable? Her tongue's a lethal weapon. Vulnerable about *what*?

JUDY: About the fact that she was a working class girl from Brunswick whose father was a labourer. About the fact that she didn't have a chance to get a decent education. About the fact that Dad's family didn't want him to marry her.

STEPHEN: You just won't face up to the fact that our mother was *malignant!*

JUDY: You just won't face up to the fact that our father was a pompous old bigot.

STEPHEN: I should have told you back then when I caught her giggling in the laundry. At least you would've understood just what was going on.

JUDY: I knew.

STEPHEN: You knew?

JUDY: I caught her out too.

STEPHEN: When?

JUDY: When I was about seventeen.

STEPHEN *stares at his sister and she nods, affirming that she's telling the truth. They remain on stage, and the focus shifts to their younger selves as we see a re-enactment of the moment when* JUDY *too became aware of the game their mother played.*

*   *   *   *   *   *

The date projected on the screen changes to 1963. We are in the living room of KATE *and* RON*'s house in Glenhuntly, a south eastern suburb of Melbourne.* KATE, *played by a younger actress than the one who plays the* KATE *we have already met, is in her early forties, slim, attractive and personable.* RON *is in his late forties.* STEPHEN *is eighteen and* JUDY *is seventeen. They too are played by actors younger than the ones playing the mature* JUDY *and* STEPHEN. *The family are all watching television. The news is being announced that the Prime Minister, Harold Holt, has decided that the new unit of decimal currency, which will be introduced in three years time, will be known as the Dollar.*

RON: That'd be right.

KATE: What would?

RON: [*disgusted*] That they'd call it a dollar. Britain gives us Shakespeare, America gives us Elvis Presley, and who do you think our government prefers? They might as well make us the fifty-first state.

JUDY: Dad will you shut up. We're trying to listen.

RON: This is my house young lady. Remember that.

KATE: [*to* RON] Britain, Britain—you're always on about bloody Britain. You've read that biography of Winston Churchill three times.

RON: He was the greatest statesman of our era.

JUDY: Churchill tried to stop us bringing home our troops from the Middle East when the Japanese were about to invade us.

RON: Rubbish! Who told you that?

JUDY: Our history teacher. Mr Mooney.

RON: I wouldn't believe anything that someone with a name like Mooney tells you about England.

KATE: We're Australians! Will you stop harping about bloody England!

RON: I'm proud to be Australian. This is the best country in the world, but only because our origins were British.

JUDY: [to RON] England grabbed every country it could and it's only just finished giving them back.

KATE: Exactly. Why don't you get off your high horse.

RON: England brought civilisation to every country it colonised. *We'd* be a lot better off if we'd stuck to being British instead of importing the refuse of Europe—

JUDY: Dad. Two of my best friends—

RON: There are exceptions, but by and large all we imported were the dregs. Yugoslavs bombing each other here in Melbourne. Bringing all their Neanderthal quarrels with them. And when I say Neanderthal I mean it. Take a close look at the shape of their heads next time you see them mangling the English tongue on television.

KATE: You'll never change him Judy. You'll never change him. [*To* RON.] Get off your damned high horse. Shakespeare! You force our drama group to do bloody *Macbeth* and nobody came.

RON: You said you wanted to play Lady Macbeth.

KATE: Our audience don't want to see people murdering each other all night. *Charley's Aunt* did three times the business of your bloody *Macbeth*. You don't know what's going on in the world Ron. You sit reading your books and when you're not doing that you're out in your shed making useless furniture that no one wants! Lucky I've got my women friends or I'd go mad.

RON: I've never met a more intellectually stunted collection of misfits in my life. [*To* STEPHEN.] Sit through an evening of their conversation and you'd risk brain damage.

KATE: At least they *have* a conversation. The only time *your* lips move is when you're reading.

STEPHEN: Will you stop it Mum. I'm trying to listen!

RON: [*to* STEPHEN] Gossip is the only currency that interests your mother.

KATE: [*to* RON] You can call it gossip. I call it taking an interest in things that move and breathe. All you ever do is read your books and glue your bloody joints.

STEPHEN: [*ashen, agitated*] Mum.

KATE: [*to* RON] You should have married your pathetic little teacher with the red hair. Deborah. You could have been two little mullygrubs together, reading Winston Churchill in bed.

STEPHEN: Mum!

KATE: [*to* STEPHEN] Take his side as usual.

RON: Will you shut up you stupid woman!

KATE: [*to* STEPHEN] See. Stupid, stupid. That's all he ever calls me. [*To* RON.] I had to leave school at fourteen because my father lost his job, *not* because I was stupid. I was top of my class. Always. The only time I've been *really* stupid was the time I agreed to marry you. I was top of my class. Always.

RON: Fat lot of competition you would have had.

KATE: [*to* STEPHEN] See? Anyone born in Brunswick had to be stupid according to your father.

RON: The reason your father couldn't get a job was that no one could ever get him out of the pub!

KATE: At least he had a bit of life in him—whenever *your* father opened his mouth the whole world yawned. And my God you inherited every last bit of his charisma.

RON: My father was a well read, dignified—

KATE: And you mother had about as much animation as an Egyptian mummy under heavy sedation, so I suppose I'm lucky you move at all.

RON: My mother was the gentlest, kindest—

KATE: Your mother was nose-to-heaven snob! She could barely bring herself to speak to me *years* after we were married!

RON: Leave her out of this!

KATE: She spoiled you rotten and pumped your head full of grand ideas about how you were going to become this and how you were going to become that, and look at you. What have you become? Nothing!

RON: You're a vicious woman with a vicious tongue.

KATE: At least my friends have got husbands who can crack a joke and make people laugh. Kid around and have some fun. I married a human blob!

KATE storms out, apparently in tears. RON is hurt and furious. JUDY leaves to comfort her mother. STEPHEN stays with his father who subsides with a long sigh back into his chair, fighting to hold back tears of hurt and anger. STEPHEN is shaken and agitated.

STEPHEN: Dad, just don't take any notice.

RON: She insults my mother, my father—

STEPHEN: Just don't take any notice.

RON: Everything my mother said about her was right and I just didn't listen.

STEPHEN wants to say more to his father but can't. He walks out of the room leaving his father alone. In the adjoining dining room, JUDY approaches her mother to comfort her but stops dead when she realises her mother is not crying but trying to stifle her giggles. KATE sees JUDY standing there with a puzzled look on her face. KATE shrugs at her daughter, inclines her head towards the living room where RON is and screws up her face in a dolorous imitation of her husband. JUDY breaks into a grin as it dawns on her what is going on.

*   *   *   *   *   *

1996. JUDY *and* STEPHEN *in their mother's living room.*

STEPHEN: You just giggled along with her? You thought it was a joke?

JUDY: Stephen, Dad needed taking down a peg or two.

STEPHEN: Sorry, I just don't find sadism amusing. And if you think it's odd I don't feel affectionate to our mother even when she's dying, that's the reason.

JUDY: Be a bit generous. Despite everything you were always her favourite.

STEPHEN: Here we go.

JUDY: You had the brains. I was just the "plodder" of the family. Dad didn't want me to go to university because he said I was only going to go and get married.

STEPHEN: He was worried about the fees.

JUDY: OK. I didn't get a scholarship like you, but at least I got honours in French, and all he said about that was that it was stupid to study French because I was never going to use it.

    Pause.

And he was right.

STEPHEN: You taught it for years.

JUDY: You *live* there and I've never even visited the place. It was *Mum* who insisted I go on to university and she went back to work full time to help pay.

STEPHEN: She wanted both of her children to have university degrees so she could lord it over her friends.

JUDY: She wanted to make sure I wasn't called "stupid" all my life like she was.

STEPHEN: She wanted us both to have degrees. She was *obsessed* with her social position—or lack of it.

JUDY: She lived through a depression in a family that had to put newspapers between the blankets to keep themselves from freezing.

STEPHEN: Her brother didn't turn out like her. She was *obsessed* with social status.

JUDY: And I wonder who took after her?

STEPHEN: [*genuinely surprised*] Me?

JUDY: Who lives in a "Chateau" in France?

STEPHEN: It's not a Chateau!

JUDY: Sorry, a Chateau "Petit". Who married a matchstick Trophy Wife half his age who'd been on the cover of *Vogue*?

STEPHEN: Yvette is far more sensitive and intelligent than you lot ever gave her credit for.

JUDY: Who has to pay double postage on every letter he writes because it takes ten pages to drop all the names?

STEPHEN: When you live in the hemisphere in which things *happen* you can't help meeting people who *make* things happen.

JUDY: Mum loves your letters. She photocopies them and sends them to all her enemies.

STEPHEN: You think *you* don't take after her?

JUDY: Me?

STEPHEN: Lethal Tongue Two.

JUDY: I call it honesty.

STEPHEN: When an Australian says, "Mate, I want to be honest with you", either punch him in the mouth or run.

JUDY: "When an Australian?" You're not one of us any more?

STEPHEN: It's taken twenty years to unlearn the grosser habits of my tribe, but I'm getting there.

JUDY: What you're getting to be, Stephen, is a total pompous prick. This is not the Australia of twenty or thirty years ago.

STEPHEN: So I keep hearing.

JUDY: It's not!

STEPHEN: It wouldn't want to be. *This* is the Australia of thirty years ago.

> STEPHEN *shows her a photo he has picked up. We see on the screen that it's a shot of* KATE *with her two friends,* CLAIRE *and* MAUREEN, *posing together in tennis gear with their racquets in hand at the Glenhuntly Tennis Club.*

Maureen and Claire. Canberra was pussy cat land compared to the politics of the Glenhuntly Tennis Club.

*   *   *   *   *   *

1965. KATE *bursts into her Glenhuntly living room followed by her two closest friends who look anxious and worried. They are* CLAIRE CUMMINS, *voluptuous and attractive, and* MAUREEN DONAHUE, *thin and febrile.*

KATE: No, Claire. I'm resigning. The Tennis Club can bloody well find another Vice President. I will not serve under that woman.

CLAIRE: If you resign Kate, Maureen and I resign.

MAUREEN: No question.

KATE: Just because she's a doctor's wife she thinks she can lord it over everyone. The truth is she's mean to the core.

KATE storms across to a drawer and pulls out a package.

This is what the lovely Jillian just gave me for my birthday. Look. The same handkerchiefs *I* gave *her* four years ago. Yellow round the edges they're so old.

CLAIRE: Mean.

KATE: Just because she's a bloody doctor's wife she thinks she's better than all of us.

MAUREEN: None of *our* husbands are fools.

CLAIRE: [*to* KATE] Your Ron's a bank manager.

KATE: He would be if he'd push himself a bit more.

MAUREEN: And he's *exceptionally* well read.

CLAIRE: He can name every play Shakespeare ever wrote.

MAUREEN: And he makes beautiful furniture.

KATE: I'm sick of tennis in any case. I've been saying for years that I want to devote more of my energy to the Dramatic Society.

MAUREEN: Kate you can't give up tennis. We'd lose every tournament.

KATE: Jillian should have thought of that before she opened her big mouth. You heard what she accused me of, I presume?

CLAIRE: [*nervously*] I didn't quite, I was—

KATE: Tell her Maureen. Tell her what that snob said.

MAUREEN: I didn't quite catch it either.

KATE: She said someone from another club complained that I used language on court.

CLAIRE: Everyone makes a slip—

KATE: I never swear on the tennis court. Never.

MAUREEN: Nobody even thinks "bloody" is a swear word these days.

CLAIRE: [*to* MAUREEN] They said Kate said, "Bloody shit."

KATE: I said, "Good hit"! Just because I grew up in Brunswick doesn't mean I've got a gutter mind. The thing she's really got against me is that I just happen to know that Lady Muck grew up in Coburg herself.

CLAIRE: Don't get too upset Kate. It'll all blow over.

KATE: I'm not going to let it blow over this time. The club elections are coming up in six weeks. I'm going to stand against her.

MAUREEN *and* CLAIRE *look at each other.*

CLAIRE: She's quite popular.

KATE: And I'm not?

MAUREEN: No. You're very popular.

CLAIRE: Very popular.

MAUREEN: Very popular.

CLAIRE: You've just made one or two enemies.

KATE: What enemies?

CLAIRE: Jillian said you've upset a few people. She asked me to stand as Vice President but of course I won't.

KATE: Upset who?

CLAIRE: You told Janice that Edith said she was a dead weight on the social committee.

KATE: She did!

CLAIRE: And then you told Edith that Janice said *she* was a dead weight.

MAUREEN: And they had a big fight and worked out who started it.

KATE: Jillian should talk. She's the worst gossip in the club. [*To* CLAIRE.] You should hear what she says about you.

CLAIRE: What?

KATE: You go ahead and stand for Vice President. I'm only too happy to stand down.

CLAIRE: What did she say?

KATE: No, it's just too nasty.

CLAIRE: What?

KATE: You stand for Vice President. I'm going to leave that club in any case. It's full of petty little snobs. I'm going to concentrate my energies on the Dramatic Society.

CLAIRE: What did she say?

KATE: You wear your neckline far too low and throw yourself at every man under ninety.

CLAIRE *stares straight ahead in shock.*

And I absolutely *won't* tell you what she said about you, Maureen.

MAUREEN: What?

KATE: No, it's appalling.

MAUREEN: What?

KATE: That you're insipid with no conversation and you shouldn't be on the committee.

MAUREEN *looks shocked.*

You want to serve under a President like that, fine.

CLAIRE: Did she really say that? About me?

KATE: Yes. And more than once.

CLAIRE: The truth is her husband made a pass at *me*.

KATE: Really. When?

CLAIRE: Just a few weeks ago. At the club dinner dance. He put his hand right—you know—

KATE: Really? I always thought he had bedroom eyes.

CLAIRE: Don't tell anyone.

KATE: Of course I won't. Of course I won't. It's just very very interesting.

KATE *stores the information. We sense she'll use it to wreak maximum damage.*

* * * * * *

1996. The action in the living room continues.

STEPHEN: At least she was even handed. She did just as much damage to her friends as her enemies.

JUDY: [*smiles*] She certainly liked a bit of infighting and intrigue. Mind you the politics where I work is ferocious and I'm just as bad as anyone. It's inevitable in any organisation.

STEPHEN: That's exactly why I swore to myself that I'd never join one.

JUDY: It's part of life.

STEPHEN: [*vehemently*] Not mine.

JUDY: You make enemies but you also get to have friends you love and trust.

STEPHEN: I wouldn't trust anyone with my garbage.

JUDY: And look where it's got you.

STEPHEN: Look where it's got me? It's got me a lifestyle I could only have dreamed about when we were kids. You think I should've spent my life gossiping and backbiting in Glenhuntly, like our mother?

JUDY: You can't isolate yourself from humanity.

STEPHEN: You can have a bloody good try.

> STEPHEN *bends down and picks up a loose photo on the floor that has caught his attention. We see on the screen that it's a shot of* KATE *with her two friends,* CLAIRE *and* MAUREEN, *at a party.* RON *is behind them all with his hands draped over* CLAIRE *and* MAUREEN*'s shoulders.*

Oh God.

> JUDY *takes the photograph and looks at it.*

JUDY: The parties.

STEPHEN: Dad used to pretend he hated them, but look at him. Drunk out of his brain having a whale of a time. Look at Claire. She was such a—

JUDY: Tart. [*Looking hard at the photo.*] That was the night that—

STEPHEN: That what?

JUDY: [*she shudders*] You really think our father was so wonderful?

STEPHEN: What?

JUDY: I ducked out of my bedroom to pinch some of the food, like we always did, and there he was in the kitchen with Claire, one hand on her bum, the other up her dress, and his—

STEPHEN: She was Mum's bridesmaid.

JUDY: Not to mention best friend.

STEPHEN: Did he see you?

JUDY: [*shakes head*] Peripheral vision is quite restricted when you've got your nose stuck in a cleavage.

STEPHEN: Especially Claire's.

> STEPHEN *frowns incredulously. They look at the photo again.*

Don't think Mum was a paragon.

JUDY: Did you ever see her doing anything like that?

> STEPHEN *looks down and finds a photo. He hands it to* JUDY.
> *It's one of* KATE *looking young and glamorous, standing by an*
> *early fifties Holden car. She's holding* STEPHEN*'s hand. He's*
> *about six years old. Behind her, with a leering look on his*
> *face, is a man with oiled hair and a sharp suit.* JUDY *looks at*
> *the photo.* STEPHEN *points to the man.*

That was her boss at Myer's.

STEPHEN: He gave us a lift to Sydney when Mum took me up to visit Uncle Stan. We stopped overnight in Gundagai.

JUDY: No woman could go to bed with someone who looked like *that*.

STEPHEN: He had a room next door to us. She snuggled close to him all next day. I can remember being really embarrassed.

JUDY: She wouldn't've.

STEPHEN: You sure?

> JUDY *frowns thoughtfully.* STEPHEN *sorts through the photos*
> *and stops at one he shows to his sister. She's standing in the*
> *quadrangle of Melbourne University in her graduation gown*
> *and mortar board, with* KATE *and* RON *on either side.*

Dad didn't want you to go to university? Look at the beam on his face the day you graduated.

JUDY: He knew he didn't have to pay the fees any more.

STEPHEN: He's proud as all get out. I was the disappointment.

> STEPHEN *hangs his head. The focus shifts to their younger*
> *selves.*

*   *   *   *   *   *

1967. RON *sits with his head hung low.* KATE *is facing young* STEPHEN. *Young* JUDY *listens in the background.*

KATE: Your father's really upset.

RON: Kate—

KATE: No, bugger him. He should know. Your father's heart was racing all last night. He's not well. You know that.

RON: Kate—

KATE: You've got one and a bit years to go and you're a *doctor*. What on earth is going on in your head.

STEPHEN: I don't want to be a *doctor*, OK?

KATE: Just explain to us why? Just explain to your parents who have made every sacrifice so that you could have a better life than they did. Just explain why?

STEPHEN: I'm just not interested in it.

RON: Not interested in healing people?

STEPHEN: No.

RON: I would have given anything to be of more use to my fellow man.

KATE: What's this ridiculous business about films? We don't even make films here? Are you going to tell us you're off to America now ?

STEPHEN: I'm not interested in the sort of films the Americans make. I'm interested in film as art.

KATE: Art? Film isn't art! Film is rubbish. Drama is art!

STEPHEN: [*flaring*] What would you know!

KATE: What would I know? I've been the leading actress at the Glenhuntly Dramatic Society for years and played some of the greatest roles ever written.

STEPHEN: Theatre's dead, and the gross overacting of the Glenhuntly Players is not about to bring it back to life.

KATE: Did you read what *The Glenhuntly Times* said about my Lady Macbeth?

KATE *searches for* The Glenhuntly Times.

STEPHEN: Theatre by definition is "Theatrical". The screen gives us integrity and truth. Haven't you heard of Truffaut, Resnais, Antonioni—

KATE: [*thrusting the review at* STEPHEN] It said that I made Lady Macbeth's ambitious villainy "chillingly real".

RON: You just played yourself.

KATE: So what do you think you're going to do?

STEPHEN: Go to Europe.

KATE: Europe?

RON: All of Europe's coming here.

STEPHEN: [*emotional*] This is the most inward looking, self centred, smug and *boring* country in the world. Have a look out the window. Twenty miles of triple fronted cream brick veneers marching across the flatness to the Dandenongs. Can't you *feel* the sterility? Can't you feel all that repressed suburban "decency"? Those aren't houses out there. They're headstones. This is the graveyard of creativity. I can't think of one interesting thing that's ever happened to me here. Right from the time I was a kid. The only thing we could think of to do on Sundays was to drive to Digger's Rest and pick blackberries.

RON: [*hurt*] You loved it.

STEPHEN: I hated it. The prickles ripped your hands apart, there were snakes in the bushes, and we had to have blackberry jam for the next bloody year.

RON: [*still hurt*] You used to run to the car. You were always the first to get in. And don't try and say you didn't like camping at Rosebud.

STEPHEN: I hated camping at Rosebud. The whole of Melbourne charged down to a forlorn stretch of shallow beach and recreated a hellish canvas facsimile of the suburbia it had just left!

RON: Bit of a selective memory there son. You used to love it so much you couldn't bear to come home.

STEPHEN: I'm not trying to hurt you Dad.

KATE: Well you are. He won't sleep a wink tonight.

RON: You used to hate having to wear shoes again. You loved the way your toes had spread like an aboriginal's.

KATE: You go off to your precious Europe. And in twenty years time when you're a nobody, don't blame us.

STEPHEN: [*to* KATE] Do you think a suburban doctor is being *somebody* for God's sake! The top French directors are treated like Gods! Dad's right, you're as thick as a brick!

RON: Don't you speak to your mother like that young lad.

STEPHEN: [*to* RON] It's exactly what *you* say.

RON: I'm her husband!

KATE: We'll see who's the smart one in the long run. You go off to Europe then Mr Big Shot. We're sick of your whinges.

RON: Kate, let's try and understand what the lad's getting at. [*To* STEPHEN.] You can't just suddenly make films. What are you going to do over there?

KATE: The same as he does here. Chase women. Use them up and dump them, that's his credo! Film, hah! All he's on about is sex and getting out on the streets waving obscene placards. Everyone I know saw yesterday's *Herald* and it's extremely embarrassing for me.

> KATE *picks up the newspaper and waves it. We see the offending photo. It shows* STEPHEN *holding up a large placard captioned "All the Way with LBJ", which shows Harold Holt unbuttoning his pants, while behind him a grinning President Johnson unzips his fly.*

Do you think the Government would send our soldiers to Vietnam if there wasn't a damn good reason?

STEPHEN: Do you *really* think we're under threat?

RON: They're got their eyes on our open spaces, don't worry.

STEPHEN: Who have?

RON: The Asians.

JUDY: Which Asians Dad? They're all different.

KATE: We wouldn't be up there fighting if there wasn't a reason. The Government knows more than you do young man.

STEPHEN: [*to* JUDY] What's the use.

KATE: Go to Europe. I'll be glad to see the back end of you.

RON: You're taking a huge risk son. If you finish medicine you'll never have to scrimp and save like we did.

STEPHEN: Dad, when I go into a theatre and see those flickering images in the dark, I come alive. My whole being comes alive. I have to start asking the big questions in the only way that has meaning to me.

KATE: What big questions?

STEPHEN: What we're doing here ? Why we exist?

KATE: Who bloody knows and who bloody cares? The fact is that we're here and we've just got to get on with it.

RON: Couldn't you just finish at uni and you'd have something to fall back on?

STEPHEN: I don't want anything to "fall back on". That's the whole point. I've got to throw myself in at the deep end and if I drown I drown—but at least I don't have to listen yet again to the only question this country ever debates—whether to buy a Holden or a Ford!

KATE: Another year and you could have had a bloody Mercedes.

STEPHEN: Can't either of you understand? Something inside me is calling and I have to follow!

KATE: I know what's calling you and it's hanging between your legs! [*To* RON.] He just thinks those French tarts are going to give him more of it than he gets here!

RON: Kate, don't be crude. He's trying to tell us something and I'm doing my best to understand.

KATE: Well when you work it out you tell me, because I just think he's crazy!

*   *   *   *   *   *

1996. JUDY *picks up another photo. It's* STEPHEN *on the quay with a ship's gangplank in the background.* STEPHEN, *cases by his side, is dressed as a Parisian intellectual already, and has a rather pained, bored look on his face.* KATE *looks tearful,* RON *looks worried.* STEPHEN *points to his sister in the photo.*

STEPHEN: You don't look very happy.

JUDY: I wasn't. You were off to France and couldn't speak a word of the language, and I was stuck out in some God forsaken outback town trying to teach it to pupils who could barely speak fifty words of *English*!

STEPHEN: You could have done what I did.

JUDY: No I could *not*. I was bonded to the Education Department to teach for at least three years! Before that was up I got married.

STEPHEN: You were never going to get married.

JUDY: Remember the times, will you. If a girl wasn't married by twenty-three she was regarded as a failed spinster or fair game. Ray helped me through one of the most stressful times of my life. I know you all thought he was dull—but he's one of the most decent men I've ever known.

STEPHEN: Don't be so paranoid. Ray is the most liked man in the history of the human species. Rabid dogs stop and lick his ankles.

JUDY: *You* thought he was boring.

STEPHEN: I like people who are boring. They make me feel adequate.

JUDY: He *isn't* boring.

STEPHEN: I'm teasing you for God's sake. Of course he isn't boring.

JUDY: You think I'm boring too.

STEPHEN: I don't think *either* of you are boring. You are a concerned, public spirited couple.

JUDY: See! You always make me feel like an earnest prig, when all I'm doing is being halfway decent.

STEPHEN: Never halfway. You are one hundred percent decent, one hundred percent of the time.

JUDY: Is there something terrible about trying to take other people's feelings into account?

STEPHEN: No, as long as you occasionally take into account your own.

> *This hits at* JUDY, *who has often felt that her selflessness is under appreciated.* STEPHEN *picks up a photo of him being welcomed at Tullamarine Airport by* RON *and* KATE.

Worst moment of my life. After six months in Europe the money ran out and they had to send me the airfare to get home. You took that shot.

JUDY: [*looking at the photo*] Then I got to hell out of there because I knew what was about to happen.

STEPHEN: I've got no recollection of that day. Mercifully it's been wiped from the memory banks.

*   *   *   *   *   *

1969. Glenhuntly. Young STEPHEN *has returned and is looking ashen as* KATE *and* RON *argue.*

KATE: Let's call a spade a spade. He's been to Europe and nobody took a damn bit of notice of him. [*To* STEPHEN.] Your father's been good enough to phone your professor and they'll have you back—so just stop all this nonsense and finish your bloody degree!

RON: He's got to want to go Kate. You can lead a horse to water—

KATE: You can lead a horse to water and if the bugger won't drink then open his mouth and shove it down his bloody throat! He's lost his scholarship and I'm willing to go back to work full time—from three days a week to five—on my feet eight hours a day—to get him through. [*To* STEPHEN.] You've had your little fantasy and you've fallen flat on your face—

RON: Kate—

KATE: [*to* STEPHEN] And don't you dare start all that banner waving again back here. I had to resign from the tennis club because I couldn't stand any more snide remarks about you.

RON: That's not why you left.

KATE: I left because Jillian told me to my face that anyone who took to the streets against the Government ought to be locked up. Doctors' wives—all the bloody same.

RON: You're obsessed with doctors' wives.

KATE: I have to serve them day in day out at Myer's and they treat me as if I'm barely human. If you'd earn enough money for us to live on I wouldn't have to put up with that sort of humiliation!

RON: You love your work. You're a top saleswoman.

KATE: Who wants to be a good bloody saleswoman when you're treated like dirt by any idiot doctor's wife you care to name? [*Pointing at* STEPHEN.] Put your foot down for once and make him go back and finish his course!

RON: It has to be his choice.

KATE: [*shaking her head in disgust*] Weak as water. You should have married that bloody schoolteacher.

RON: I wish I had.

KATE: Would have been perfect for you. She had about as much personality as a fish head. "Deborah".

RON: At least she didn't have a vicious streak a mile wide like you.

KATE: [*to* RON] When God was handing out spark, she was at the back end of the queue. [*To* STEPHEN.] You just get and finish medicine!

STEPHEN: No!

KATE: [*to* STEPHEN] You went to Europe and nothing happened and now you've just got to stop dreaming and get on with your life.

STEPHEN: I went to Europe and saw that they were just people like any other people. We've got our own stories to tell.

KATE: I thought you said that nothing ever happened here.

STEPHEN: We love, we hate, we grieve like everyone else. Gorton's starting a film school, and at the next election when Whitlam gets in—

KATE: Whitlam? That sonk. He couldn't get in a bath without drowning.

STEPHEN: —the arts are going to help define what it is that we are and I'm going to be part of it.

KATE: Finish your degree and then you can be part of the Great Wall of China for all I care.

RON: Your mother might be right son.

KATE: Get back to university!

STEPHEN: No!

>STEPHEN *storms out.* KATE *looks at* RON.

RON: We did out best.

KATE: You? What did you do? You did bloody nothing!

RON: I'm going—

KATE: Yes, go on. Out to your shed. Make some more bloody cabinets. The world can't wait. Meanwhile your son goes and ruins his life.

RON: The boy must decide for himself!

*   *   *   *   *   *

1996. STEPHEN *picks up a photo from the floor. It's their mother on stage with the rest of the cast. The stage has a rudimentary proscenium arch.*

STEPHEN: Oh God. The Glenhuntly Dramatic Society.

JUDY: The only place there was no drama was on stage.

STEPHEN: Actually Mum was the only actor with talent amongst the lot of them.

JUDY: Maybe we thought she was so good because the others were so bad.

STEPHEN: [*indicating the photo*] No she was good. Bloody good. I saw this play. It was the first thing they took me to.

JUDY: [*trying to remember*] What was it called?

STEPHEN: No idea.

*   *   *   *   *   *

1958. RON *is directing a rehearsal involving* KATE, CLAIRE, *and* MAUREEN. KATE *certainly has her agenda, but her demeanour is more one of mischievous fun and disruption than malevolence.* RON *in contrast is inclined to be pompous and self righteous. They are doing Terence Rattigan's* French Without Tears. KATE *is playing Diana and* MAUREEN *is playing Jacqueline. The others sit around watching, waiting for their turn.*

RON: Now let's try that again. Kate—there's no need to stick the pin into Maureen so hard.

KATE: It makes it look more real.

RON: That might be true, but we don't want Maureen's arm to end up like a pin cushion.

KATE: She's as tough as they come, aren't you Maureen?

MAUREEN: [*nervously*] I don't mind if it makes it look more real.

RON: All right but you don't need to do it in rehearsals.

KATE: Maureen—can I just make a suggestion here? You're supposed to be in love with Kit—and furious that I'm moving in on him—right?

MAUREEN: Right.

KATE: You're doing it *very* well, and I know the character you're playing is *very* polite—but it might be better if there was a little bit more anger bubbling away under the surface.

MAUREEN: Isn't it showing?

KATE: Well, yes, but—

RON: You're doing fine Maureen.

MAUREEN: You can't tell? That I'm angry underneath?

RON: Of course we can. Maybe just give us a tiny bit more. Can we do it again?

> *The two women assume their roles:* KATE *as Diana and* MAUREEN *as Jacqueline.*

MAUREEN: I've got something to say to you, Diana. Do you mind if I say it now?

KATE: Of course not. [*Tugging* MAUREEN*'s dress.*] Oh Lord, there's a bit of braid coming off here.

MAUREEN: Oh.

KATE: I'll fix it for you.

MAUREEN: If you look in that basket over there you'll find a needle and thread.

KATE: Right.

MAUREEN: But you needn't trouble—

KATE: That's all right. It's no trouble. I enjoy doing this sort of thing. [*Threading needle.*] Well, what was it you wanted to say to me?

MAUREEN: I overheard your conversation with the Commander this afternoon.

KATE: [*making a shot with the thread. She turns to the light*] All of it, or just part of it?

MAUREEN: I heard you say you were in love with the Commander and that you didn't love Kit.

> KATE *jabs the needle in with relish.* MAUREEN *jumps.*

Ow!

KATE: Sorry darling, did I prick you?

MAUREEN: Are you going to tell him?

Left to right: Max Gillies as Ron, Melissa McMahon as Judy (younger),
Anthony Weigh as Stephen (younger) and Carol Burns as Kate (younger)
in the 1997 Queensland Theatre Company production. (Photo: Rob MacColl)

Left to right: Max Gillies as Ron, Carol Burns as Kate (younger) and
Sally McKenzie as Maureen in the 1997 Queensland Theatre Company
production. (Photo: Rob MacColl)

KATE: Now let's be honest for a moment. Don't let's talk about love and things like that, but just plain facts. You and I both want the same man.

MAUREEN: Kit? But you don't—

KATE: Oh yes I do.

MAUREEN: But what about the Commander?

KATE: I want him too.

MAUREEN: Oh.

KATE: [*as* KATE] Not Oh, Maureen. Oh! You're shocked. Oh! Oh!

RON: Kate, I'm directing.

KATE: Then direct! It's Oh! Not Oh.

MAUREEN: Oh.

KATE: Oh! Oh!

RON: Kate—

MAUREEN: Oh!

KATE: That's better. [*As Diana.*] Don't look shocked, darling. You see, I'm not like you. You're clever. You can talk intelligently, and you're nice. You have been sent into the world with lots of gifts, and you make use of them. Well, what about me, with just my one gift? I must use that too, mustn't I?

MAUREEN: Well, what you call my gifts are at any rate social. Yours are definitely anti-social.

KATE: Oh, I can't be bothered with that. The fact remains that having men in love with me is my whole life. It's hard for you to understand, I know. You see, you're the sort of person that people *like*. But nobody *likes* me.

MAUREEN: I wouldn't mind if everybody hated me, provided Kit loved me.

KATE: You can't have it both ways darling. Kit looks on you as a very nice person.

MAUREEN: Oh God. What I'd give to be anything but nice.

KATE: [*doing her line in the way it should be done*] Oh God! What I'd give to be anything but nice!

RON: Kate, I'm directing.

KATE: So you keep saying. The text says she says the line "with sudden anger".

MAUREEN: [*trying again*] Oh God. What I'd give to be anything but
   nice.

KATE: Oh God! What I'd give to be anything but nice!

MAUREEN: [*distressed*] I can't do it.

KATE: Yes you can!

     KATE *jabs her with the needle again.*

MAUREEN: [*angry*] Oh God! What I'd give to be anything but nice!

KATE: [*as herself*] Beautiful. Well done. Let's take a break.

RON: Let's take a break.

MAUREEN: Was that really all right?

KATE: Really good.

     MAUREEN *gravitates to* RON, *who reassures her.* KATE *heads*
     for CLAIRE.

She's hopeless. You should be playing that role. I told Ron right
   at the start.

CLAIRE: She's getting better.

KATE: She's hopeless. How's the audience ever going to believe that
   Kit falls for her? There's no spark. Nothing. If you were playing
   it I'd have some competition.

     KATE *pats* CLAIRE *reassuringly and goes across to intercept*
     RON *as* CLAIRE *goes across to talk to a still distressed*
     MAUREEN.

She's hopeless.

RON: [*defensively*] All right. All right. We'll switch roles and have
   Claire play the part. That's the way I always wanted it.

     KATE *does a swift calculation. Does she want the*
     competition?

KATE: No. Claire would be too obvious.

*   *   *   *   *   *

1996. STEPHEN *puts down the shot of* French Without Tears.

STEPHEN: I don't think it's my memory playing tricks. I really think
   she had talent.

JUDY: It's a pity there wasn't any professional theatre around when she was young.

> STEPHEN *looks at his sister and nods. It's something he's never thought about before.* JUDY *picks up a cuttings book.*

I didn't know Mum kept a book of your cuttings?

STEPHEN: She didn't. Dad did.

> *We glimpse fleetingly newspaper articles of* STEPHEN*'s early documentary film successes. An article about the first of them is headed "Macrae hits a nerve with 'The Acid Test'" and suggests that the documentary asks pertinent questions about whether the counterculture is about more than pot and LSD. The second headline, "Macrae does it again with 'Feet on the Streets'", which is said to capture the wave of revulsion that brought hundreds of thousands out on the streets to protest about the Vietnam War. An article dated 1974 features a double page spread on* STEPHEN *with a large photo of him sporting a beret and black leather. Its heading is "Lasseter's story makes it to the big screen".* STEPHEN *tries to take the book off his sister before she can turn the next page, but it's too late. The headlines read "Lasseter or Lassitude?", "Lasseter's gold lacks sparkle", "Limping Lasseter's last crawl". The glimpses of text we read are cruel in their demolition of the film, using adjectives like "turgid", "tedious", "pretentious", and "a travesty".* JUDY *looks at* STEPHEN. *It's obvious the memory still hurts.*

JUDY: Critics.

STEPHEN: They were right.

> JUDY *looks at him.*

JUDY: It had a lot of good things in—

STEPHEN: It was a bad movie.

*   *   *   *   *   *

1974. STEPHEN *is seething with anger.* RON *listens with concern.* KATE *is more impatient.*

STEPHEN: Are they all blind? Lasseter's journey is a metaphor for Australia's journey into its own psychic interior.

RON: Don't let the ignorance of a handful of third rate journalists deter you son.

KATE: It *was* a little slow.

RON: I didn't find it slow.

KATE: No you wouldn't. [*To* STEPHEN.] My friends did find it a little slow.

STEPHEN: An epic journey has to take time.

RON: Those desert vistas were magnificent.

KATE: It could have had a bit more going on.

STEPHEN: It isn't a soap opera!

RON: [*to* KATE] It was a wonderful achievement, and you should be very proud.

KATE: If you cut about twenty minutes out of the middle it might do better.

STEPHEN: Mum—the middle section is what *generates* the metaphoric power.

KATE: The only thing it generated in me was a sore behind. But don't listen to your mother. I know nothing. I've only been the backbone of the drama society for the last twenty years.

RON: Winston Churchill—

STEPHEN: [*to* KATE] This is a film about hopes, dreams, obsession, disillusionment, and despair. If I wanted petty interpersonal bickering I'd just set up my camera in your living room!

RON: Winston Churchill—

KATE: Shut up about bloody Winston Churchill!

RON: Winston Churchill had to live through what he called his "Wilderness Years". Right through the thirties. Everyone said he was finished—

STEPHEN: Nobody's saying I'm finished.

KATE: Just read the papers again.

RON: Kate!

KATE: He's got to face facts. [*To* STEPHEN.] You think your mother's stupid, but I'm not. You want to know what was wrong with your film? It had no passion. It had no characters who loved or hated or laughed or cried.

Pause, then gently.

I'm not trying to be cruel love, but it was as obvious as Paddy's pigs that there was no drama. Now for God's sake, for your own good and not mine, go back and finish medicine.

STEPHEN: No!

*   *   *   *   *   *

STEPHEN *closes the cuttings book. The memory is still painful.*

STEPHEN: I watched the film again the other day and Mum was absolutely right.

JUDY: What did she say?

STEPHEN: No drama. And I suddenly realised why—twenty years too late. I hated conflict. It reminded me of them.

JUDY *looks at him.*

I'll go and sit with her tomorrow. You have a rest.

JUDY: I won't exactly be having a rest. I'll start sorting through all her clothes and belongings.

STEPHEN: Sorry, I keep forgetting—you have never allowed yourself an idle moment in your life.

JUDY: Look don't get righteous because you finally take a little bit of the load. I've been looking after the two of them for years. You didn't even come back for the funeral when Dad died.

STEPHEN: What was the use? He was dead.

JUDY: Mum needed to know that you cared. About her.

STEPHEN: I don't! I used to read novels about sons loving their mothers and shake my head in bewilderment.

JUDY *looks at her brother reproachfully.*

I'll sit with her tomorrow.

*   *   *   *   *   *

STEPHEN *approaches his mother's bed in the hospital. He's not sure whether she's awake or not. He sits by her bed.* KATE *is sleeping, but suddenly opens her eyes.*

KATE: Do you love your mother?
STEPHEN: [*struggling*] Yes, of course.
> KATE *stares at him, then sighs and sinks back into her pillow.*

KATE: You were always the favourite. Always. With your father *and* me. Judy knew. That's why she hates me.
STEPHEN: She doesn't hate you.
KATE: Oh yes she does. Can't wait to see me go.
STEPHEN: She's very upset.
KATE: I bet.
> *Pause.*

Your father and I gave you everything and you couldn't even come back for his funeral.
STEPHEN: I'm sorry.
KATE: [*sighs*] Play the record. Third track.
> STEPHEN *goes across to find the record.*

Palais de Dance. Burnt down now.
STEPHEN: Sorry?
KATE: I met your father at the Palais de Dance. In St Kilda. Big bands. They used to play real music. Not like now.
STEPHEN: I didn't know you met at a dance hall.
KATE: Where else could a girl from Brunswick meet a boy from Ormond? He came there with his mousy little schoolteacher. Deborah. I spotted him across the hall and I thought, "He's wasted on that little ferret." She didn't have a chance.
STEPHEN: Dad's family wanted him to marry her didn't they?
KATE: Tried every trick in the book, but she didn't have what it takes.
STEPHEN: What did it take?
KATE: What do you think? Men are all the same.
> *Pause.*

It was a hollow victory though.

STEPHEN: What do you mean?

KATE: Your father never loved me. All he loved was the bloody sex.

STEPHEN: I'm sure that's not true.

KATE: Oh it's true all right. That's all he ever wanted out of me finally.

STEPHEN: No.

KATE: Men might have some extra bits on the outside but there's a huge piece missing inside. I had to rescue you from some disasters your crotch was leading you into. Remember that dancer? I fixed her.

STEPHEN: Fixed her?

KATE: I rang her and told her that if I saw her again I'd bend a golf club around her skull. I want you to spread my ashes with your father. You hear?

STEPHEN: You just said he didn't love you.

KATE: Maybe he did. In this situation you start giving the benefit of the doubt. I want you to promise to take the ashes. Your sister will promise and won't.

STEPHEN: She will.

KATE: No, you do it. I want to be sure. You can just hang around here and not jet off back to Yvette. You can stay and do something for your mother.

STEPHEN: I will, I've told you.

KATE: Neither of you love your mother. Neither of you give a damn.

STEPHEN: We do.

KATE: I bet. So are you happy over there? Got everything you want?

STEPHEN: Yes, it's fine.

KATE: Plenty of money?

STEPHEN: Comfortable.

KATE: Comfortable? Don't give me that. You're rolling in it. Not that your father or I ever saw a penny of it. How rich are you?

STEPHEN: Money is not my prime concern. I've just been offered three hundred thousand U.S. dollars to shoot a commercial in the Philippines but I'm turning it down.

KATE: Why?

STEPHEN: Cigarette companies can't advertise in the West any more so they're targeting the third world poor.

KATE: Better not tell Yvette you turned it down.

STEPHEN: I'm sure she'll agree.

KATE: I bet.

STEPHEN: [*tersely*] You want some music?

KATE: Yes, put on the music. Here comes the morphine. Pity you have to be dying before they let you have this stuff. Third track. This is the song that was playing when we had our first dance.

> STEPHEN *puts it on. We hear "After the Ball is Over". His mother begins to sing along but fades off to sleep.* STEPHEN *sits there listening.* KATE *opens her eyes.*

Do you love your mother? Really?

STEPHEN: [*emotional*] Of course.

KATE: Don't lie to me son. I need to know.

STEPHEN: Of course I do.

KATE: If you don't then no one does.

STEPHEN: Of course they do.

KATE: No. If you don't, no one does.

STEPHEN: Of course I do.

KATE: You're not lying? Really?

STEPHEN: No.

> KATE *looks at him then sinks back into the pillow .*

KATE: I'll never really know will I? That's the awful thing about life. You never really know.

> KATE *sinks further into the pillow and goes to sleep.* STEPHEN *sits there watching her and listening to the music.*

END OF ACT ONE

ACT TWO

1996. STEPHEN *returns to his mother's place to find his sister* JUDY *sitting in a chair, drinking red wine.*

JUDY: How's Mum?

STEPHEN: She keeps asking me...

JUDY: What?

STEPHEN: To play that awful song. "After the bloody ball". I try get to sleep and that bloody song keeps yonking along in my brain. "So many hearts they are broken, Af-ter the ball." Not working?

JUDY: I found the dozen French reds you sent. They've never been touched.

STEPHEN: They have now.

JUDY: Yeah, bugger it. Do you think I *like* being Goody Two Shoes?

STEPHEN: What is it?

JUDY: [*reads the label*] Chateau Latour.

STEPHEN: I sent them a case of Chateau Latour and they didn't drink it? Do you know how much that stuff is worth?

JUDY: An absolute *fortune*, I'm sure. It's nice to have a relative to whom money is no object.

STEPHEN: Here we go.

JUDY: Living in the South of France.

STEPHEN: Why is it such a huge problem for you that I live abroad?

JUDY: What's so wonderful about France?

STEPHEN: [*pointing to the Chateau Latour*] That's a start. How is it?

JUDY: It's fucking brilliant. I've never tasted anything remotely like it. Bastard! Ray and I have to think twice before we buy a bottle of bloody Jacob's Creek!

STEPHEN: You and Ray have other satisfactions. Working to help disadvantaged minorities.

JUDY: Yeah and it pays us shit.

STEPHEN: [*looking at the bottle*] It's a great year.

JUDY: And it's Mum's, so I get six bottles.

STEPHEN: Five.

JUDY: You wouldn't give me the lot as a gift, would you? Typical.

STEPHEN: Have them. I'll deduct the market price from your share of the estate.

JUDY: You would too.

STEPHEN: I don't want you and Ray to have your integrity challenged by affluence.

JUDY: You know I—no.

STEPHEN: What?

JUDY: No, I'm drunk. I'll start to say things I shouldn't.

STEPHEN: Start?

JUDY: Ray said to me—no.

STEPHEN: Go on.

JUDY: Ray said to me. Your brother is so wealthy that he *might*—he *might*—

STEPHEN: Give you all Mum's money?

JUDY: We have only been out of this country twice in our lives. Once to Vanuatu, where Ray caught dengue fever, and once to India where we both got the shits. I have never ever been to France and I speak the language!

STEPHEN: No one would understand you. Your accent's appalling.

JUDY: I told Ray that you'd grab every bit of your half even though you haven't done a thing to help the parents for twenty years.

STEPHEN: For Christ's sake I'm not that rich that I can throw away— sixty thousand or so!

JUDY: You earn a fortune.

STEPHEN: Do you know how expensive France is?

JUDY: I know how expensive it is if you're living in a Chateau and drinking Chateau Latour.

STEPHEN: Our house is not a Chateau.

JUDY: It's got sixteen rooms and four full time fucking servants!

STEPHEN: Three!

JUDY: Sorry, "three". Your daughters all have their own horse, and riding lessons, and clothes that must cost—

STEPHEN: I work hard for my money. It's my business how I spend it.

JUDY: The only time my kids ever rode a horse was a pony ride at the zoo.

> JUDY *picks up a photo which shows Yvette, in a very expensive dress, standing in a smart apartment.*

And this is your little Paris pad.

STEPHEN: Yvette's friends are in Paris.

JUDY: And you support her parents as well? You've been suckered Stephen. That menagerie will keep you on the commercial treadmill until you're seventy-five. Your new movie will never get made because you can't afford to take the risk.

STEPHEN: It was never going to get made in any case.

JUDY: The script is really good.

STEPHEN: It's hopeless. I wrote it during a brief bout of homesickness.

JUDY: It's good. And for *me* to admit that, means it's probably *fantastic*.

STEPHEN: Do you think I want to go through the "Lasseter" fiasco again?

JUDY: That script is *fifty* times better than "Lasseter". It's got passion.

STEPHEN: Who wants to see a film about an Australian convict who finally grew some wheat?

JUDY: It's not about that. It's about how England dumped people here they thought were the dregs of humanity, left them without resources or food, and how they survived to eventually found the first true democracy in the planet's history.

STEPHEN: The rest of the world will yawn.

JUDY: I don't think so. Come out here and make it. Couldn't you drag yourself away from the Gallic Wafer for just six months?

STEPHEN: Do you have to be so *nasty* about Yvette?

JUDY: She's using you. You're her magic pudding. The more she spends the more there is.

STEPHEN: [*tersely*] Believe it or not we fell in love.

JUDY: I'm amazed how "falling in love" always happens at such a convenient time. She was never a top model, her career was just about over, the family trucking business went bankrupt—

STEPHEN: We fell in love.

JUDY: Her family treat you like dirt and so does she. When you're not dropping names your letters make pretty sad reading.

STEPHEN: I exaggerate that side of it when I'm feeling down.

JUDY: She's had a series of affairs—-

STEPHEN: I don't know that for sure.

JUDY: If I found a letter addressed to Ray that said he was hotter than a bowl of red chillies, I'd suspect he wasn't just running a temperature.

STEPHEN: [*anguished*] For God's sake I love the woman, and I certainly love my kids!

JUDY: Stephen, she cheats on you, she makes fun of you in front of her friends, and she hasn't earned a franc for well over ten years!

STEPHEN: She brings up the kids!

JUDY: So what do the nanny and housekeeper do?

STEPHEN: She needs time for her painting.

JUDY: I've seen her painting. That'll earn you heaps. Stephen, you've been suckered. Admit it. You were so besotted with anything French you would have married a baguette. And you have. Even though you're an arsehole you're still my brother and I care.

> JUDY *is silent. She looks away.*

STEPHEN: Mum wants her ashes spread with Dad's.

> JUDY *stares at him.*

JUDY: What?

STEPHEN: [*nods*] It took him fifty-five years to escape.

JUDY: I'm not doing it this time. It's 500 kilometres or more. Why in the hell does she want her ashes up there?

STEPHEN: God knows.

JUDY: You can take them.

STEPHEN: Drive to East Gippsland? I have to be in the Ph—in Spain in just over a week.

JUDY: You do it or it doesn't get done.

STEPHEN: I'm not even sure why *Dad* wanted his ashes there. We only went there once.

> JUDY *knows. She picks up an album and finds a photo which she shows him. It's a shot of a young boy of about thirteen holding up a fish next to a rowboat by a river. Next to him* RON *stands beaming.*

JUDY: That's why.

> JUDY *looks at the photo of* STEPHEN *and* RON *by the rowboat.*

Parenthood is a giant swindle. You put up with all the agonies of the early years thinking there's finally going to be a payoff of warmth and affection, and it happens for three days between the ages of thirteen and fourteen.

STEPHEN: Better let me have all that Chateau Latour. It only depresses you.

JUDY: I'm not taking those ashes up there again.

STEPHEN: She's never going to know, is she?

JUDY: Stephen!

STEPHEN: I simply haven't got time.

JUDY: Let it be on your conscience then. I'm not doing it.

> *She swigs the last of the Chateau Latour.* STEPHEN *picks up a newspaper cutting. It's a shot of* STEPHEN *at a political rally. His hair is long and this time he's carrying a banner through the Melbourne streets which has a photo of Malcolm Fraser with a Hitler type moustache drawn in on it. Under the photo is the caption "Kerr's Cur".*

STEPHEN: Mum didn't have much luck with my press appearances, did she.

> *He hands the photo to* JUDY.

* * * * * *

1975. Glenhuntly. KATE *and* RON *are upset. Young* STEPHEN, *his hair long as in the photograph, is trying to be conciliatory, but finding it hard.*

KATE: You're going overseas *permanently*? That's ridiculous. You can't just change countries.

STEPHEN: Mum, now that Malcolm Fraser's taken over it's the end of everything here. Film, the arts—everything.

KATE: We hardly ever see you now and you live in the same bloody city. Your father gets really, really hurt—did you know that?

RON: Kate—

KATE: It's about time he knew. It's about time he knew. Your father was sitting there with tears in his eyes the other night. You know how long you haven't rung for? Nearly two and a half weeks.

RON: Kate—

KATE: I let things out, but your father hurts inside.

RON: Kate—

STEPHEN: I'm sorry, I've been extremely busy.

KATE: Now we know why. Getting ready to pack up and leave. Turn your back on your family, your country—not caring a damn how many people you hurt on the way.

RON: Kate—

STEPHEN: A duly elected Government was sacked by the Queen's representative. We're a bloody colony and we always will be!

KATE: That's just an excuse.

STEPHEN: Excuse?

KATE: You got a hard time over your film so you're running away.

STEPHEN: When one of the top critics in France declares your film a masterpiece, and all that happens back here is that the press continues to *torment* you, then it doesn't exactly endear you to the place!

KATE: What about Simone eh? What about her feelings?

STEPHEN: Simone and I weren't serious.

KATE: Really? Well you tell Simone that. I had her on the phone a few weeks back crying her eyes out.

STEPHEN: What she needs is a steady guy in a steady job—family—

KATE: Don't you ridicule people who raise families my boy. Your father held down a steady job all his life. Hated it. Hated every minute of it. Your father had capabilities far beyond adding up figures in a ledger, but he stuck at it, and why?

RON: Kate—

KATE: I'll tell you why. To provide a decent home for you two. And look where it's got him.

STEPHEN: Exactly!

KATE: He doesn't regret a minute of it. Or he wouldn't if he had children who appreciated all he's done.

STEPHEN: Mum, this isn't even a democracy any more. The Queen's representative—

KATE: He had tears in his eyes the other night. He said, "Where did I go wrong." He said that that last holiday we went on to Bemm River was the last time you've ever said a kind word to him.

RON: Don't embarrass the boy Kate!

KATE: You were out in the little rowboat and you put your arm around his shoulder and said, "It's a great holiday Dad."

RON: Kate please.

KATE: He treasures that. In a whole lifetime, "It's a great holiday Dad" is all he's ever had. And now you're packing your bags, never to be seen again. What a wonderful son.

STEPHEN: Dad, I'll be back. Often.

RON: She's exaggerating son. I was just a little bit down.

STEPHEN: I'll be back. The jets these days—twenty-four hours and you're home.

KATE: [*tears starting to form in her eyes*] Don't you think *I'm* going to miss you? It's not just your father. *I'm* going to miss you.

STEPHEN: I'll be back.

KATE: Do you think parents don't care? Do you know what I went through to have you? Thirty-two hours in labour? The doctors warned me against it. Time and time again they warned me. "Don't do it. Your kidneys can't take the punishment." And I should have listened.

RON: Kate don't—

KATE: I should have bloody well listened. We might as well not have had him for all the pain he's caused.

STEPHEN: Mum, you're not being rational.

RON: She rarely is.

KATE: [*in tears, to* RON] You want me to have no bloody emotions like you?

RON: I've got emotions but I can control them.

KATE: That's your bloody trouble isn't it? Never show anything to anyone and load all your private hurts on me? What am I supposed to do? Our son is just running off as if we mean nothing to him, and I'm supposed to smile and wave him goodbye.

STEPHEN *moves across to try and comfort his crying mother. She shoves him aside.*

Don't try and smoodge up to me. It's too late for that. You've been a bitter disappointment to your father and I, and just you remember that.

STEPHEN: [*losing his temper*] I've got to do what I think is best for my life! Can't you understand that!

KATE: Best for *your* life. Yes I can understand that perfectly.

RON: Don't take too much notice of your mother son. She's upset.

KATE: And *why* am I upset? Because of him! The Queen didn't get rid of that no hoper Whitlam. We voted the bugger out. Of course this is still a democracy. You're leaving because of the bloody film!

STEPHEN: [*to* KATE] A horrific political act has been perpetrated on this county and you can't even see it! Well I can, and I can see what happens around here too!

KATE: Around here? What happens around here.

STEPHEN: You make Dad's life miserable and everyone else's life miserable just for the hell of it!

KATE *stares at him in shocked silence.*

RON: That's a bit strong son.

STEPHEN: Is it?

KATE: My life has been *lived* for your father and you kids. That's my problem. Everyone else comes first.

STEPHEN *realises that his mother really believes this about herself. There's nothing he can say.*

STEPHEN: Sorry but I have to go.

STEPHEN *embraces his father, hugs his sobbing mother, who this time doesn't shrug him off, and he turns and leaves.*

*   *   *   *   *   *

1996. STEPHEN *picks up a photo of his mother looking very attractive in her younger days.*

STEPHEN: She's started asking me if I love her and it makes me break out in a cold sweat. I want to say yes. I want to mean it at least once before she dies.

JUDY: She hasn't asked me.

STEPHEN: She knows you do. Can you remember something— anything our mother ever did for anyone else out of sheer generosity or compassion?

JUDY: She went back to work full time when her kidneys were giving her hell so that you and I could go to uni.

STEPHEN: Someone outside the family.

JUDY: When's the last time *you* did anything for anyone outside your family?

> STEPHEN *wheels around and looks at his sister. She's hit home again.*

Maureen told me a few years back that Mum not only got Claire and her a job at Myer's, she went right out on a limb when the management tried to sack them.

STEPHEN: I bet.

JUDY: I don't remember the details, but I believe her.

*   *   *   *   *   *

1979. Myer's department store. MAUREEN *is crying.* CLAIRE *is looking distressed.*

CLAIRE: He can't do that.

MAUREEN: He did. Bang. Just like that.

CLAIRE: Did you tell him *why* you have to sit down now and then?

MAUREEN: No.

CLAIRE: Maureen, you should've!

MAUREEN: He didn't give me time. He just walked up and said, "You've been warned. Go and get a week's pay and get out of here."

CLAIRE: He can't do that.

MAUREEN: "Go and get a week's pay and get out of here." And he turned and walked off.

> KATE *arrives with a grim look on her face.*

CLAIRE: Mr Clark sacked her.

KATE: Mr Clark? That kid in the office?

CLAIRE: For sitting down when there wasn't a customer in sight.

MAUREEN: I *never ever* sit down when there are customers around.

KATE: That kid in the office whose mother still packs him a playlunch?

CLAIRE: "Get a week's pay and get out." Just like that.

KATE: [*eyes glinting*] We'll damn well see about that!

MAUREEN: Don't do anything Kate. He'll sack you too.

KATE: Be buggered he will. What's his bloody name again?

MAUREEN: Don't Kate.

CLAIRE: Clark.

> KATE *looks up and bellows in the direction of* CLARK's *office.*

KATE: Mr Clark! Mr Clark! Just come here a minute please.

MAUREEN: Don't Kate. He'll sack you too.

KATE: It's about time someone reminded the KGB who makes the profits around here.

> MR CLARK *comes across to them. He's a smart young manager who is played by the same actor who plays the younger* STEPHEN. *His manner is officious and cocksure.*

CLARK: Yes, Mrs Macrae?

KATE: Did you just give Maureen a week's notice?

CLARK: Yes.

KATE: When she's worked here twenty-six years without a break?

CLARK: She's been warned four times not to sit down on the job.

KATE: Have you ever spent eight hours on your feet at her age? Have you?

CLARK: Look I'm not going to enter into any discussion about this matter.

KATE: You are not going to "enter" into any discussion? Well I'm sorry you have just "entered" into discussion. I asked you if you've ever spent eight hours on your feet and I'll tell you the answer—

MAUREEN: Kate—

KATE: The answer is no, you haven't. You sit on your bum for eight hours a day in your bloody office and spy on us! She only sat down for a few minutes when there were no customers in sight.

CLARK: It is strictly forbidden—

KATE: She's old enough to be your mother young man! You put her back on staff straight away. She knows more about cosmetics than any other person in this store!

CLARK: Who do you think you are?

KATE: Who do I think I am? I'm someone who's worked here for thirty years on and off, and every year I have worked I've topped the sales figures for whatever department I've worked in. That's who I am.

CLARK: You just better watch your tongue or you'll find yourself out of here too.

KATE: Don't be too cocksure of yourself young fella, I've got friends a lot higher up than you in this store. Do you want me to go and see Mr Mulvaney?

CLARK *looks a little unsure of himself for the first time.*

CLARK: She was warned four times.

MAUREEN: Kate, don't get yourself involved.

KATE: I've known you since we were in State school. You don't think I'm going to let this little pipsqueak lord it over you. You just put her back on the payroll straight away, or I'm going straight to Mr Mulvaney.

CLARK: He'll back me up. And if you don't get back to work, you'll be fired too.

KATE: Go on. Fire me. Let's see how far you get.

MAUREEN: Kate.

KATE: No, bugger him. How dare he.

CLARK: How dare you speak to me like this.

KATE: Why—because you've got a bloody diploma or something? My daughter's got a PhD! Put Maureen back on staff or I'm going to Mr Mulvaney right now to tell him that if Maureen goes, all of us go.

    CLAIRE *nods her head in agreement.*

CLARK: Mr Mulvaney will back me all the way. He's the one who told me to crack down hard.

KATE: Listen young man and listen carefully. You don't "crack down hard" on a woman that has given this store twenty-six years of dedicated service. A woman who has a severe bunion problem but is too proud to ask for special treatment. A woman whose husband is on an invalid pension and relies on her wage. A woman who can still outsell any young airhead around here you care to name. Now if you want me to see Mr Mulvaney—who is a *very* good friend—He often gave me lifts to Sydney and back— then I will see Mr Mulvaney—but if he finds out you are responsible for the loss of three of his best staff, then I wouldn't like to be in your shoes.

CLARK: [*to* MAUREEN] You didn't tell me you had bunions.

MAUREEN: You didn't give me a chance!

CLAIRE: You didn't give her a chance!

CLARK: Then get them bloody well treated, and don't let me catch you sitting down again.

KATE: She will sit down when she has to sit down if there are no customers around. Don't you try and bully her!

CLARK: All right! Do what you like! Sit down, lie down, just leave me alone!

    He storms off. The three women embrace each other, elated.

* * * * * *

1996. JUDY *is at her mother's bedside in the hospice.* JUDY *thinks her mother is asleep but she's not.*

JUDY: Why do you want your ashes up in Bemm River, Mum? You didn't like it at all when we went.

KATE: The best thing about heaven is there'll be no mosquitos. That buzz in the dark. They didn't touch your father. Just me. Nothing ever touched your father.

JUDY: Why do you want your ashes with Dad's?

KATE: We were married for fifty-five years.

> *There's a silence. She closes her eyes.* JUDY *thinks she's asleep and goes to get up.*

Stephen won't do it. You and Ray were always good to us. Stephen couldn't have cared less.

> *There is another pause as* KATE *fights to stay conscious.*

Your brother's very smooth, but he's got no principles. Just about to shoot a cigarette commercial in Asia for three hundred thousand U.S. dollars.

JUDY: That's appalling. The cigarette companies pay off corrupt governments because they can't advertise any more in the West.

KATE: For a few days work.

JUDY: That's appalling.

KATE: Always out for the main chance, your brother. No loyalty to anyone. Certainly not his parents. You'll take my ashes up to be with your Dad, won't you?

JUDY: It'll be done.

KATE: Play track three.

> JUDY *goes across and plays "After the Ball is Over."*

* * * * * *

1996. JUDY *enters the living room.*

STEPHEN: How is she?

JUDY: Not much change.

Pause.

Stephen when you leave here, where are you going?

STEPHEN: To Spain.

JUDY: To shoot a commercial for what?

STEPHEN: For some er—hair shampoo.

> JUDY *looks at him, then at a photo* STEPHEN *has picked up of he and Yvette.*

[*noting the photo she is looking at*] I made a special trip out here to tell them about Yvette and all I got was abuse.

*   *   *   *   *   *

1983. RON *and* KATE *are in their living room.*

RON: I just naturally thought he'd bring her out with him. I thought he'd have wanted us to meet her.

KATE: You tell *him* that.

RON: I will.

KATE: No you won't. You'll leave it to me to do your dirty work as usual.

RON: I'll tell him.

KATE: Then *do* it for once. You're upset, I'm upset—why shouldn't he know.

> STEPHEN *enters after having put down the phone. It is eight years since we last saw him and from this point in the play the two older actors playing* STEPHEN *and* JUDY *play their younger selves.*

STEPHEN: That was Ray. Judy's on her way.

> *Pause.*

I'm sorry Yvette had to cancel the trip, but she's very very busy.

KATE: Modelling?

STEPHEN: Photographic modelling. She's very sought after.

> KATE *looks at* RON, *signalling him to say something. He doesn't.*

KATE: Your father's—

RON: Don't bring me into this. If she's busy she's busy.

STEPHEN: She really wanted to come.

RON: [*looking at a photo*] She's certainly a very attractive woman, son.

STEPHEN: She's a terrific person.

KATE: So are we *ever* going to get to see her?

STEPHEN: Of course. We'll be out as soon as we can.

> *The doorbell rings and* JUDY *comes in carrying a salad. Brother and sister embrace, but relatively stiffly.*

JUDY: I believe congratulations are in order.

STEPHEN: Yep. It finally happened. Has Mum shown you the photo?

JUDY: Yes. She looks very young.

STEPHEN: Is that a tone of disapproval?

JUDY: Surprise.

KATE: She'll have you on the hop my boy.

JUDY: She's a model?

STEPHEN: Photographic. Speaks four languages.

KATE: You wouldn't put her on the phone because you said she didn't speak English.

STEPHEN: She doesn't.

KATE: Well what does she speak? Swahili?

STEPHEN: Spanish, Italian and German.

RON: So you speak together in—

STEPHEN: French.

KATE: So your children are never going to speak English?

STEPHEN: Oh yes. I'll make sure of it.

RON: I hope so. The language of Shakespeare is a priceless gift. Not that we'll hear it in this country much longer.

JUDY: Dad, no more of that stuff please. You're as bad as that bigot Geoffrey Blainey.

RON: I think what he said was totally sensible.

STEPHEN: Sorry, who is—

JUDY: An academic who made a public speech saying that the pace of Asian immigration was "too fast".

Left to right: Max Gillies as Ron and Bille Brown as Stephen (older) in the 1997 Queensland Theatre Company production. (Photo: Rob MacColl)

RON: He didn't say they shouldn't be coming here. He just said the pace is too fast.

JUDY: Dad, twenty years ago you were carrying on about how terrible it was that we were taking in the dregs of Europe. Now your beloved Carlton footie team is peppered with Silvagnis and Motzerellis and it's all fine.

RON: Be a long time before we get a blessed Vietnamese on our forward line. They just don't mix.

JUDY: Dad, we helped rip their country apart.

RON: Name me one Asian country that's a true democracy. They have a different mind set.

JUDY: Dad, don't get me angry. We've finally discovered that we're geographically part of Asia and not a moment too soon.

RON: [to STEPHEN] She's learning Vietnamese.

JUDY: And Indonesian.

STEPHEN: Indonesian?

JUDY: I don't approve of what happened in East Timor, but I can understand.

STEPHEN: Explain it to me.

JUDY: Look, I'm committed to a new vision of what this country could be and I'm excited by it— [To STEPHEN.] What are you grinning at?

STEPHEN: Vietnamese *and* Indonesian. You never do things by half.

JUDY: The problems and challenges of Australia wouldn't mean much to an international sophisticate like you.

STEPHEN: Loosen up.

JUDY: You mightn't be so "loose" if you came home occasionally and did your fair share of looking after your parents.

KATE: Looking after? We're not invalids.

JUDY: [to STEPHEN] I've got an extremely demanding new job. It's not just a matter of teaching English. The kids I deal with are refugees who have been through traumas we can't begin to understand.

KATE: We're not—(invalids).

JUDY: [to STEPHEN] Ray or I have to ferry Dad to hospital two or three times a week—

RON: If it's too much trouble—

JUDY: Frankly Dad, it is a *lot* of trouble. It's not just the hospital visits. I'm over here at least four or five times a week—to take Mum shopping—to bring the kids because there's all hell to pay if we miss a Sunday—

KATE: They're our grandchildren.

RON: The doctor said there's a chance I could get my licence again after the next operation.

JUDY: Oh Dad, be realistic. You've had a major heart attack, you're riddled with arthritis, and your eyesight is so bad you'd be lethal. Mum should learn to drive.

KATE: I'm too old to start learning things like that.

JUDY: Well Ray and I can't keep it up.

KATE: I would have thought your parents occasionally took precedence over your bloody Vietnamese.

JUDY: I think it's time you both faced the fact that you'd be better off in a retirement village.

KATE: I wouldn't be seen dead in a village.

JUDY: Ray and I can't keep doing this any longer.

STEPHEN: If they don't want to go, you can't force them.

JUDY: Good. Then *you* come home with your child bride and do your share. I even have to come over to give Dad his injections because *she* can't face it.

KATE: I can't handle needles and things like that.

JUDY: [*to* STEPHEN] And have him at *your* house when she goes on bowls tournaments.

KATE: I'm President of the club.

RON: Not for much longer. If you spread poison eventually they work out where it's coming from.

JUDY: [*to* KATE] Your friend Maureen's in an excellent village down Dromana way and says she's very happy.

KATE: Maureen'd be happy in a tea chest at the tip.

JUDY: She says that there's a very good bowls club there.

KATE: They're always having to stop matches because some old biddy drops dead on the green.

JUDY: Mum, I'm sorry. If you won't take responsibility for Dad, then there's no other option because I can't any longer and he [*She points to* STEPHEN.] won't.

KATE: He's not my bloody responsibility. I've got a life of my own.

RON: I don't want to be anybody's responsibility!

JUDY: Unfortunately Dad, you are.

STEPHEN: Mum, you did take certain vows. For better or for worse.

KATE: Yes, well I didn't know what a lifeless blob he was going to turn out to be, did I? You try living with someone who sits there day in day out reading the large print version of *David Copperfield four* times!

RON: It's Charles Dickens' great masterpiece.

KATE: I'm not wasting my life on him.

RON: I've wasted mine on you already.

KATE: See. Never a civil word.

JUDY: I'm not wasting my life on the both of *you.* If you weren't my bloody parents I wouldn't come within a hundred kilometres of here.

KATE: Great thanks for all we did for you.

JUDY: You represent everything that makes my flesh creep about this country.

STEPHEN: Judy, steady on.

JUDY: [*to* STEPHEN] You look after them! [*Pointing at her mother.*] She's so bloody self centred and lazy she won't even cook meals for him. I have to feed him as well.

KATE: He doesn't want much these days.

JUDY: White bread and Vegemite? She can't even be bothered toasting it!

STEPHEN: Mum, do you care about Dad at all?

RON: Of course she doesn't. Never did. Just wanted to grab me off Deborah.

KATE: Deborah would have left you years ago, you blob. No one in the history of the world has read *David Copperfield* four times.

STEPHEN: I'm going to a hotel and taking the first plane out of here.

JUDY: Don't you dare run off the minute you get here. They're your responsibility as much as mine.

STEPHEN: It was a huge mistake coming here and it's a mistake I won't make again for a long while.

JUDY: You're just a shit. A self centred irresponsible shit just like her!

KATE: That's a fine way to talk about your mother.

RON: Don't go off again son. You've barely said hello.

STEPHEN: Sorry Dad, but this sort of bickering is the very reason I got out in the first place.

JUDY: That's fine for you. I feel the same way but I've got to face it.

STEPHEN: [*exploding*] Mum, you're going into a retirement village and that's it!

STEPHEN *moves towards the door and turns.*

Just do it! Judy's had enough of you and so have I.

He leaves.

KATE: Why did I ever have children?

*   *   *   *   *   *

1996. JUDY *picks up a photo of* RON *and* KATE *standing outside their neat little house in a retirement village.*

STEPHEN: Thank God I forced the issue.

JUDY: *You* forced the issue?

STEPHEN: Told them they had to go to a retirement village.

JUDY: You flew in, went white, and flew out again. I had to coax them for months.

STEPHEN: All right. I did nothing,

JUDY: The irony is that when they finally did go, Mum loved it. You don't know what politics is until you've been in a retirement village.

STEPHEN: That's why they all live so long. They can't bear to miss out on the latest gossip.

Pause.

Look I know I didn't do my share with the parents and I know what a strain it must have been for you and Ray.

JUDY: It wasn't fun.

STEPHEN: So I'm sorry. I just couldn't face it.

JUDY: I had no choice.

> STEPHEN *turns away from her guiltily and picks up a photo of he and Yvette standing with* KATE *and* RON *outside his parents' retirement villa in 1988.*

STEPHEN: When I did bring Yvette and young Angelique all the way out to see you all in 1988, you made us feel as welcome as lepers.

*   *   *   *   *   *

1988. CLAIRE *and* MAUREEN *are fussing around* KATE, *helping her into her fifty year old wedding dress. They are already in their bridesmaids' gear, although in their case the actual dresses they wore have long since disappeared. In* CLAIRE's *case this is probably just as well as we suspect that she might have had difficulty squeezing into the original.*

MAUREEN: I think it's extraordinary. Fifty years on and she hasn't put on an ounce.

KATE: Just don't ask me to breathe.

CLAIRE: How many are coming Kate?

KATE: Just about everyone.

MAUREEN: Valerie told me that Majorie Stevens is furious.

KATE: Good. She might ask herself why she didn't invite Ron and I to *her* fiftieth anniversary.

MAUREEN: Be fair Kate. You'd just arrived.

KATE: We'd been here four months.

CLAIRE: Wilma's a little hurt too.

KATE: Well maybe she shouldn't have made such a fuss because the *one* packet of biscuits she bought at our fundraising stall was *one* day out of date.

> RON *comes in wearing an old suit that is patently too tight. He has trouble walking these days, and has a pronounced limp.*

RON: Do we have to do this?

KATE: Will you bloody well stop whingeing. Claire has come all the way from the Gold Coast.

CLAIRE: Wouldn't miss it.

MAUREEN: It's so romantic Ron. Kate'll be walking down the aisle in the *same* dress with the *same* bridesmaids—

RON: Towards the same unfortunate victim.

KATE: Put a smile on your face for once in your life and pretend you aren't miserable.

RON: The suit's too tight. I look stupid.

KATE: Don't blame the suit.

>STEPHEN *and* JUDY *come in.* JUDY *is carrying a tray of food.*

JUDY: You look beautiful Mum.

KATE: Not too bad for an old girl, am I? [*To* STEPHEN.] Where's Yvette and little Angelique?

STEPHEN: Angelique's sick. Yvette's looking after her.

>KATE'*s expression indicates that she doesn't believe a word of it.* JUDY *notes the look and cuts in.*

JUDY: And you look good too Dad.

RON: I look ridiculous.

KATE: You won't get a smile out of the blob.

>KATE *waits until* RON *has just lowered himself with effort into a chair.*

Get off your bum and put some music on.

RON: I just sat down.

STEPHEN: I'll do it Dad.

RON: [*getting up*] No, you sit down and relax.

>RON *moves towards the CD player.*

JUDY: [*to* KATE] The prawns looked so good I got an extra half kilo. [*To* CLAIRE *and* MAUREEN.] Don't you two look stunning?

CLAIRE: Not bad for a pair of old matrons are we?

JUDY: Lovely day for it too.

>RON *puts on the record. It's Mantovani and, as a result of* RON'*s failing hearing, it's very loud.*

KATE: Turn it down!

STEPHEN *hastily moves in behind his father and turns it down.*
KATE *waits until* RON *has just settled in his chair again.*

For God's sake Ron. Not Mantovani. Something more lively.

RON: What?

KATE: You choose.

RON: I just sat down.

STEPHEN: [*getting up*] I'll do it.

RON: No, you relax son.

> STEPHEN *looks anything but relaxed as* RON *struggles to his feet again.*

[*to* KATE] What do you want?

KATE: You choose.

RON: Whatever I choose it'll be wrong. What do you want?

> STEPHEN *gets up from his chair and picks out a CD.*

STEPHEN: [*to* KATE] Frank Sinatra?

KATE: Perfect. See Ron. It's not that hard.

> STEPHEN *puts the record on softly.*

RON: Frank Sinatra. No voice at all compared to Bing Crosby. If it wasn't for his Mafia connections we'd never have heard of him.

> KATE *waits until* RON *has just sat down again.*

KATE: Put the kettle on Ron. People would like a cup of tea.

STEPHEN: I'll do it Mum.

KATE: Let him do it. Never gets off his bum.

RON: I'm up and down like a bloody yo yo. [*To* STEPHEN.] She does it all the time.

KATE: If I didn't, you'd sit there for weeks on end.

STEPHEN: Still reading a lot Dad?

> RON *is preoccupied working the remote control of his television.*

KATE: You have to yell, he's as deaf as a post. He can't even read big print these days. He just sits staring at whatever's on the bloody television. [*To* RON.] Turn it off. You've got guests.

RON: I haven't got the sound on.

KATE: Turn it off!

RON: The tall ships are coming up Sydney Harbour.

KATE: Bloody Bi-Centenary. Who cares when Captain Cook arrived?

RON: It was Captain Phillip!

KATE: Who cares?

RON: You wouldn't. You know nothing about your country's history or anything else.

KATE: Turn that television off!

> RON *sits there defiantly, staring at the screen.*

[*to* STEPHEN, *getting tearful*] I can't deal with him. I can't deal with him any more. He sits there day in and day out watching dry as dust ABC documentaries and football replays. Day in, day out. It's like living with a corpse.

RON: You're just ignorant woman. Ignorant. If I watch something with substance it's far too boring for your mother. This country's being ravaged by greed and ignorance and your mother doesn't want to know.

KATE: Bloody ABC. Bloody "Four Corners". They carry on as if everyone in Australia is a crook. Alan Bond's a crook, Robert Skase is a crook—

RON: It's Christopher Skase, you stupid woman!

STEPHEN: Dad—

KATE: Alan Bond's a personal friend of Bob Hawke. Do you think our Prime Minister would be friends with a crook!

RON: This country's being plundered by thieves and all your mother does is gossip on.

KATE: Bloody ABC. I'd ban it.

RON: Yes, you would you stupid woman!

STEPHEN: [*distressed*] Look will you two just stop it! This is supposed to be a celebration of fifty years of marriage.

JUDY: [*to* STEPHEN] Welcome home.

KATE: [*tearful*] I can't handle him Stephen. I just can't handle him.

CLAIRE: Let's all have a drink. That'll fix things.

RON: Just because I like to use my mind.

KATE: And don't get him started on the Asians.

RON: Let them flood in and take over the country. Who cares?

JUDY: Dad, don't. Please.

KATE: [*to* JUDY] He just does it to get you upset.

RON: [*to* JUDY] Don't you get a little worried when your daughter brings home her school photo and half the faces are Asian?

JUDY: Dad, you're being stupid and racist.

RON: I'm not racist. A racist believes his lot's superior. I don't. *They're* superior. Year after year the top students are always Asians.

JUDY: Their culture encourages achievement.

RON: Culture my eye. Asians are brighter than whites. In fifty years time all we'll be doing is collecting their garbage.

KATE: He's such a bloody embarrassment. If I do manage to get him to step outside the door, you can't shut him up.

RON: [*to* JUDY] Your daughter's birthday at that Chinese restaurant. Fourteen of us—and that waiter remembered *every* order without even writing it down. No white could do that.

JUDY: Dad, if you don't stop I'm leaving.

KATE: Stop? Course he won't stop.

RON: Why should I—all I'm doing is telling the truth. The aboriginals treated this land well for forty thousand years then we came and ruined it in two centuries, but it's nothing to what the Asians are going to do when they take over. Two thousand miles of high rise. Surfers Paradise from Adelaide to Cape York.

STEPHEN: Dad, calm down. You're celebrating fifty years of marriage.

RON: [*points to* KATE] She couldn't give a damn about the marriage. She just wants to show off the fact that she can still get into her wedding dress.

KATE: We're going down to the centre. If you want to come, come. If you don't I couldn't care less.

She moves towards the door, followed by CLAIRE, MAUREEN *and* JUDY.

MAUREEN: Cheer up Ron.

RON: What's to cheer up about? Fifty years of disaster.

KATE: You're not kidding. [*To* STEPHEN.] See what I've got to put up with?

Left to right: Max Gillies as Ron, Bille Brown as Stephen (older) and Carol Burns as Kate (younger) in the 1997 Queensland Theatre Company production. (Photo: Rob MacColl)

RON: [*to* STEPHEN] Your mother and I are like oil and water, chalk and cheese.

KATE: [*to* RON] If you want to come, come. If you don't no one will miss you.

MAUREEN: Cheer up Ron. Have a drink.

KATE: A drink? You'd need a bomb to get him moving. Leave him. At least *we'll* enjoy ourselves. Just like the old times!

> KATE *turns up the volume of the amplifier to very loud and begins to sing along with Frank Sinatra who is singing "The Lady is a Tramp". She turns it into a very polished and funny song and dance routine as she heads for the door.* MAUREEN *and* CLAIRE *applaud her exit and follow her.*

JUDY: [*taking the food dish*] I'll go and help with the food.

> *She goes.* STEPHEN *turns down the volume of the amplifier.* RON *sits in a chair staring straight ahead.*

STEPHEN: Dad, why don't you go out more. Make some friends?

RON: Friends? In this place? There are a hundred and seventy women and six surviving men. And they're all mental pygmies. You know why men die young? So they don't have to put up with women.

STEPHEN: Dad, what's happening between you and Mum is awful.

RON: It's always been awful. That's why you ran away.

STEPHEN: It's got worse.

RON: This country worries me more than your mother. When you and your sister were little tots we could let you play right up and down Camden Street and we knew you'd never come to any harm. Everyone in the street trusted each other. We had plumbers, milkmen and managers and there was no envy because we all earned roughly the same. Graeme Atkins two doors up turned down a five quid a week rise—and that was a fortune in those days—because he didn't want to become a foreman and lord it over his mates. Unthinkable today now the fast buck is the only reality.

STEPHEN: You and Mum should never have got married.

RON: If I had my time over I suppose I'd have to do it again.

> STEPHEN *looks at him in surprise.*

I couldn't bear to think of a world without you and your sister in it.

STEPHEN: We haven't exactly—

RON: Your kids are your kids. You always love them.

Pause.

Look I'm sorry about your mother and I. There's too much bad feeling for it ever to be lovey dovey again I'm afraid. Any rate, it won't be long now before she's rid of me.

STEPHEN: Dad—are you—

RON: Yes?

STEPHEN: Scared. Of dying?

RON: You're joking. The arthritis in my back is so bad now that every single day of my life is agony. I wake up in the morning praying that this day will be my last.

STEPHEN *puts his arm around his father's shoulder, fighting the tears in his eyes.*

When I die, look in the inner flap of my wallet. You'll understand things more then.

Pause.

Now, we better go to this blessed circus or your mother will make my life even more miserable.

STEPHEN *helps his father to his feet.*

*   *   *   *   *   *

1996. STEPHEN *turns to* JUDY. *He's suddenly remembered something.*

STEPHEN: Did you ever look in Dad's wallet when he died?

JUDY: No. Why?

STEPHEN: What happened to it?

JUDY: The wallet? [*She points to a steel box.*] It'll still be in there with his papers. Mum kept everything.

STEPHEN *rummages inside the box, takes out the wallet and looks in the inner flap. He takes out a photo and shows* JUDY. *It's a shot taken over sixty years ago of a pretty young girl smiling shyly at the camera in an open field.*

Who is it?

STEPHEN: Has to be her. The schoolteacher. Deborah.

JUDY: He carried it round all his life?

STEPHEN *nods.* JUDY *looks back at the photo.*

The old bastard.

STEPHEN: I think it's sad. He probably *would* have been much happier.

JUDY: [*nods*] Another mismatch like our parents would defy the laws of probability.

Pause.

I guess I shouldn't've given Dad such a hard time. The country just changed too fast for him. He came from an era when everyone was called Smith, Macrae or O'Connor and lived behind a picket fence in a sterile suburban wasteland.

STEPHEN: It's a rather nice picket fence *you've* got in Hawthorn.

JUDY: Hawthorn's quite ethnically diverse these days.

STEPHEN: Really? Lots of Vietnamese?

JUDY: Some.

STEPHEN: That restaurant you were telling me about?

JUDY: What are you trying to say Stephen?

STEPHEN: Have you ever thought of living in Footscray instead of just teaching there? You could practise your Vietnamese every day and it would save all the travelling to work.

JUDY: You think you're so smart.

STEPHEN: It's an exciting and bustling community so I hear. A bit of a problem with drugs and gangs—

JUDY: Exaggerated by the press.

STEPHEN: —but you still don't want to put the family at risk. It makes perfect sense.

JUDY: They're living together to preserve a cultural tradition that we're not part of. We'd just be interlopers.

STEPHEN: You wouldn't be welcome?

JUDY: We would be welcome. It just wouldn't be appropriate.

STEPHEN: So what's the future of this country? Lots of enclaves where it's not "appropriate" to live.

JUDY: We've invited people from Asia to come and live with us, and we can at least be sensitive to the fact that despite the glories of European culture, they might prefer to retain their own.

STEPHEN: Stick in your own little tribe?

JUDY: Everyone needs to feel they belong to a cultural tradition.

STEPHEN: Why? All that tribalism has ever done for the world is generate war and hatred. And you've adopted it as a national policy.

JUDY: We can't force them to belong to *our* tribe.

STEPHEN: Why does anyone have to belong to any tribe? We're just about to enter the twenty-first century and finally come to terms with the fact that we're all citizens of one world.

JUDY: Not everyone can be part of an international elite Stephen. We can't all prostitute our skills to the highest bidder like you!

STEPHEN: Prostitute?

JUDY: Cigarette commercials for Asia?

STEPHEN: Did Mum tell you that?

JUDY: Three hundred thousand U.S. for a few days' work?

STEPHEN: The evil old witch. I turned it down. I told her. A few days off death and she's *still* stirring up trouble!

JUDY: Citizen of the world? You're as tribal as any of us. You're frantically trying to reattach yourself to the European tribe your ancestors left four generations ago. And you're doing it because you can't face up to what you really are—a bloody Australian like the rest of us!

STEPHEN: Why in God's name would I want to live here in a country that suddenly feels it has to turn its back on the greatest artistic heritage in the history of the world?

JUDY: No one's asking anyone here to turn their back on Europe— just to acknowledge that there are other traditions and cultures.

STEPHEN: And none of them come anywhere *near* what Europe has achieved. Why would anyone *not* want their children to grow up there rather than here?

JUDY: Because for no good rational reason some of us love this country—its light, its landscape, its space, its tolerance—

STEPHEN: Tolerance? Pauline Hanson?

JUDY: She's not going to win! She's like our father. Living in the past! This country is on its way to becoming something new. Not European, not Asian, not anything other than itself and I want to be around to help make that happen!

STEPHEN: Good luck to you. I'll just continue to eke out a miserable existence looking down the Dordogne Valley drinking Chateau Latour.

JUDY: You go back and live your pretend life in your pretend marriage—

STEPHEN: What entitles you to make judgements like that!

JUDY: Read your own letters! The parts you ask me not to pass on to Mum. If you were honest with yourself you'd admit Yvette is a vain, stupid woman who bores the shit out of you!

STEPHEN: Not true!

JUDY: Read your own letters. Carefully. You're fond of your kids, sure, but as far as human bonds go that's it!

STEPHEN: I've got tons of friends. Tons. I speak perfect French and I'm totally accepted.

JUDY: I've got *real* friends. Friends who'd do anything to help me if I was in real trouble. I could name twenty. Let's hear your list.

STEPHEN *tries to come up with names but can't.*

You were teased in the schoolyard, and you saw our mother teasing Dad, so you decided the world was cruel and heartless and shut down all real connections!

STEPHEN: Give us a—(break)

JUDY: You saw our mother teasing Dad—

STEPHEN: [*angry and upset*] She wasn't *teasing*, she was *tormenting*! She was *tormenting*.

JUDY: They were *wrong* for each other. That's all. It happens. It doesn't mean that all people are tormentors. Most people are decent—

STEPHEN: Sure.

JUDY: —decent, compassionate and kind. Show vulnerability and they'll embrace you, not torment you. You've wasted your whole life!

STEPHEN: No!

JUDY: Yes! Face yourself Stephen. You've wasted your whole bloody life!

> *She turns away in anger and goes off to bed, leaving* STEPHEN *stricken, with tears in his eyes.*

*   *   *   *   *   *

STEPHEN *walks into* KATE*'s room at the hospice. She is breathing in long strained gasps. It's an effort.*

STEPHEN: How are you doing Mum?

KATE: Not good.

STEPHEN: You're looking fine.

KATE: No I'm not, and neither are you. Judy giving you a hard time?

STEPHEN: She's so *critical* of my life. Over there.

KATE: So she should be. You're not happy are you?

STEPHEN: Everybody has difficulties.

KATE: That bloody Yvette.

STEPHEN: [*irritated*] Yvette isn't the problem! It's the things I miss *here*. Gum trees, beaches, Wilson's Promontory, the Great Ocean Road, the colours of the Barrier Reef, the light, the air. The easy self deprecating way Australians can send themselves up. Even football—a friend sends me over tapes of the Carlton matches. Yvette stares at the game in horror—"C'est l'anarchie!" I say, "C'est Australien."

> STEPHEN *picks up a photo that is by* KATE*'s bed. It's a photo of his father and mother, hand in hand looking young and happy.*

KATE: You *are* going to take my ashes up there to be with him aren't you?

STEPHEN: Mum, you *hated* each other.

KATE: No.

STEPHEN: Once, when I was about eleven...

KATE: What?

> STEPHEN *hesitates.*

What?

STEPHEN: I saw you picking at him until he totally lost it, and you ran into the laundry and you were—*laughing.*

KATE: It was like a devil in me.

> *Pause.*

The sex was good afterwards.

> STEPHEN *stares at his mother.*

Is that why you never loved your mother? Because you knew I liked niggling him when I was bored?

STEPHEN: He was hurt.

KATE: So was I when he kept calling me stupid. The poor bugger's career was such a fizzer he had to feel superior to someone.

> STEPHEN *stares at his mother. He looks at the photo again.*

STEPHEN: I used to stare at this photo for hours when I was a kid. Trying to work out where it was taken so I could go and stand on the *one* spot on the face of this globe where you both, at least for an instant, *seemed* happy.

KATE: [*indignant*] We were! You don't think we started out hating each other for God's sake.

> *Pause.*

I really loved him at the start.

> *She pauses to gain her breath, and sighs.*

He used to be so bloody handsome.

> STEPHEN *stares at his mother. The possibility that they did love each other at the start has never occurred to him. He moves to her and holds her hand but she is already asleep.*

* * * * * *

JUDY *sits by her mother's bed.*

KATE: You're here.

JUDY: I'm here.

KATE: Stephen's not happy.

JUDY: I know.

KATE: Are you? Have *you* got what you wanted out of life?

JUDY: No, not entirely.

KATE: What have you missed out on?

JUDY: Excitement, I guess. And love.

KATE: Love? From me you mean?

JUDY: I'm sorry, this isn't the time.

KATE: You're not going to get another chance.

JUDY: The kids I teach—when we finish the course we hug each other. There's warmth. With you—

KATE: I hate fuss.

JUDY: Fuss.

KATE: You know why you haven't had any excitement? Because you've got no guts. You married Ray because you were scared no one else would come along.

JUDY: Ray is fine.

KATE: I said "Go overseas", "Fall in love", "Don't get married too young like I did." Isn't that what I said?

JUDY: Ray *loved* me!

KATE: So did I. I just didn't *fuss* about it.

JUDY: You certainly didn't.

KATE: If you were unhappy you should have said something.

JUDY: You can't ask for love!

   Pause.

I always did so *much* for you, but it was clear that—

KATE: Stephen was the favourite. Get it out of your system.

   There's a pause as KATE *fights for breath.*

I mightn't have fussed, but I loved you. Maybe not as much as Stephen, but I did. Parents always love their kids. It's the way it is. Ah, there goes the morphine. Wonderful stuff. You still feel the pain but it doesn't seem to matter.

She drifts off to sleep. JUDY *watches her.*

* * * * * *

1996. The retirement village. Late at night. STEPHEN *puts the phone down and turns to* JUDY *who appears in her dressing gown.*

STEPHEN: The nurse says the breathing pattern is getting ominous.
JUDY: How ominous?
STEPHEN: She's not sure. I'll go. If it starts looking bad I'll call you.
JUDY: I'd better come too.
STEPHEN: If it looks bad I'll call you.
JUDY: I'd better—
STEPHEN: You need some sleep. I'll call. As soon as the phone rang that bloody song started blitzing my brain again. "Many the hopes that have vanished, After the ball." It's colonised my unconscious. For the rest of my life no more Beethoven, no more Brahms, whenever a snatch of music floats into my mind it's going to be "After the bloody Ball!"
JUDY: Call me the minute...
STEPHEN: Of course.

* * * * * *

1996. The hospital. In the early hours of the morning. STEPHEN *arrives. A young* NURSE, *played by the actor who played young* JUDY, *is listening to* KATE's *laboured breathing pattern.*

NURSE: Sorry, but I think it's very close.
STEPHEN: Oh God, will you ring my sister?
NURSE: I have. She's on her way.
STEPHEN: Thank you.
NURSE: If you need me, press the button.

The NURSE *leaves.*

STEPHEN: Can she still hear?

STEPHEN turns to receive a reply from the NURSE *and realises that she's not there. He turns back to his mother.*

No, I don't suppose you can. No matter. I'll still put on your favourite song.

He goes to the CD player and puts on "After the Ball" softly. He takes his mother's hand.

Does that take you back? The Palais de Dance? Big bands? Streamers? Polished floors? Swirling dresses? The nervous banter? The sizing up? The quickening heart beat as eye caught eye across the crowded floor? And Dad? You'll be with him again soon.

KATE *emits a sigh.*

You *did* love him at the start, didn't you? That's why you want your ashes up there with him. Nobody starts a relationship thinking it's going to be anything less than perfect and neither did you. On the Richter scale of marital discord yours would have scored in the very high sevens, but I've finally realised that it wasn't your fault and it wasn't his. In another country and another time your talent *would* have been spotted and you *wouldn't* have spent your life angry and bored. Doctors' wives would have filled theatres and given you standing ovations. You would have got the love and attention you craved—and probably deserved.

Pause.

Do you know why I think Dad left his Deborah for you? I don't think it was the sex. I think that deep in his bones he knew you were the most talented person he was ever going to meet in his life. But you made him pay. An audience of one was never going to be enough for you, was it? I'm not condemning. I finally understand. And I'm really sorry. Just when I *can* say I love you and mean it, it's too bloody late.

KATE *breathes a long, satisfied sigh.* STEPHEN *frowns and turns as the* NURSE *comes in.*

Can she still hear?

NURSE: Possibly. Hearing's the last thing to go.

She goes. STEPHEN *turns back to his mother.*

STEPHEN: I'll take your ashes up to be with Dad. The water will bubble and fume and you'll both be at it again for all eternity, but I'll do it, so don't feel you have to hang on. It's too hard now and too painful. Go peacefully. Please. Go peacefully.

KATE: [*with a great struggle*] Yes.

KATE *takes two more short breaths and stops breathing.* STEPHEN *stares at his mother and breathes his own sigh of relief that her ordeal is over.* JUDY *hurries in wearing her dressing gown. Brother and sister look at each other.*

* * * * * *

The next morning back at the retirement village STEPHEN *gets off the phone and turns to* JUDY.

STEPHEN: Monday morning at eleven. OK?

JUDY: Fine. I'll start ringing around in just a minute.

STEPHEN: I'm staying on to take her ashes up to Bemm River.

JUDY: Don't you have a shoot to do? In Spain?

STEPHEN: It was the cigarette commercial in the Philippines. I've cancelled.

JUDY: Postponed?

STEPHEN: Cancelled.

JUDY: I'm sorry I was so angry at you the other night.

STEPHEN: You were right. I asked myself who my real friends were, and came up with the answer, zero. I asked myself what I felt really strongly about, and came up with the answer, nothing. I asked myself if there was anyone in the world who loved me and came up with answer, zilch.

JUDY: One, at least one.

She hugs her brother.

STEPHEN: You're right. I've wasted a life.

JUDY: It's not over yet.

STEPHEN: When I was a kid there were things I used to look forward to so much I couldn't bear the wait. Christmas, holidays at Rosebud, a film that was coming to our cinema—now there's absolutely nothing that I look forward to—nothing.

JUDY: Make your film.

STEPHEN: I can't. I couldn't bear another "Lasseter".

JUDY: You've spent half your life honing your cinematic skills—

STEPHEN: Making junk.

JUDY: Then stop making junk. You said the Film Corporation guaranteed you half the budget just on the basis of the script.

STEPHEN *nods and permits himself a half smile.*

STEPHEN: You'll never guess what tune's bopping away in my brain?

JUDY: She's sending you a message.

STEPHEN: What?

JUDY: [*in her mother's voice*] "I'm dead, you're next. Get on with it."

STEPHEN: Do you think it really *is* a story that—?

JUDY: Yes, I do, but I could be wrong. It could be a flop that'll make "Lasseter" look like "Citizen Kane".

STEPHEN *looks at her.*

You'll be vulnerable, but you'll be alive.

JUDY *goes leaving* STEPHEN *alone on the stage. We suspect he's still hearing "After the Ball" in his head.*

THE END